DK EYEWITNESS

T0001485

TOP 10
MARRAKECH

Top 10 Marrakech Highlights

The Top 10 of Everything

CONTENTS

Marrakech Area by Area

Streetsmart

Within each Top 10 list in this book, no hierarchy of quality or popularity is implied. All 10 are, in the editor's opinion, of roughly equal merit.

Title page, front cover and spine *Jemaa el Fna square lit up at dusk, Medina*
Back cover, clockwise from top left *Ceramic bowls; Majorelle Gardens; Aït Benhaddou; Jemaa el Fna; Koutoubia Mosque*

The rapid rate at which the world is changing is constantly keeping the DK Eyewitness team on our toes. While we've worked hard to ensure that this edition of Marrakech is accurate and up-to-date, we know that opening hours alter, standards shift, prices fluctuate, places close and new ones pop up in their stead. So, if you notice we've got something wrong or left something out, we want to hear about it. Please get in touch at **travelguides@dk.com**

Welcome to
Marrakech

An age-old trading post, Marrakech is easily accessible from Europe. The city has an almost mythical quality, its pink ramparts dramatically backed by the purple peaks of the Atlas Mountains, while the spiced air of labyrinthine alleys lends an aura of magic and mystery. With DK Eyewitness Top 10 Marrakech, this vibrant city is yours to explore.

At the heart of the medieval walled Medina is **Jemaa el Fna**, a vast plaza filled with mesmerizing sights, from musicians and acrobats to fragrant street food stalls. It is the ideal spot from which to start exploring. To the south is the **Kasbah**, an area rich with palaces and tombs; to the north are the bustling **souks**, where almost anything can be bought, from herbal remedies to kaftans and carpets.

Outside the fortified gates, the **New City** districts of Guéliz and Hivernage offer orange-tree-lined avenues with a wealth of chic dining, drinking and shopping spots as well as cultural experiences. One of the area's unexpected delights is discovering the lush and colourful gardens, notably the **Majorelle Gardens**.Marrakech makes a splendid base for exploring southern Morocco. Hop on a bus or hire a car to experience the blue-and-white charms of the Atlantic port of **Essaouira**. Alternatively, head south to the **mountains** and to the **desert** beyond for imposing tribal fortresses, oasis villages, dune seas and a centre of international cinema.

Whether you're coming for a weekend or a week, our Top 10 guide brings together the best of everything Marrakech has to offer. The guide has useful tips throughout, from seeking out what's free to places off the beaten track, plus eight easy-to-follow itineraries designed to tie together a clutch of sights in a short space of time. Add inspiring photography and detailed maps, and you've got the essential pocket-sized travel companion. **Enjoy the book, and enjoy Marrakech**.

Clockwise from top: **Jemaa el Fna**, **Riad Kniza**, **the port at Essaouira**, **Kasbah Aït Benhaddou**, **tile detail at Medersa Ben Youssef**, **a Marrakech carpet souk**, **gardens in La Mamounia Hotel**

Exploring Marrakech

Marrakech may be low on museums and monuments, but a visit here is all about soaking up the atmosphere and culture. Even so, there are a handful of places that should not be missed. Four days allows you to see the best of the city and gives you time to make a day trip south into the mountains.

Key
— Two-day itinerary
— Four-day itinerary

Medersa Ben Youssef is one of the most beautifully decorated buildings in the city.

Two Days in Marrakech

Day ❶
MORNING
Start at Jemaa el Fna (see pp12–13), then head to the **Saadian Tombs** (see p68). Have a leisurely lunch at **Café Clock** (see p71).

AFTERNOON
Head over to the **Badii Palace** (see pp30–31), then return to Jemaa el Fna (see pp12–13) by one of the rue Riad El Zitouns. Take a stroll to the famous **La Mamounia Hotel** (see pp34–5) for an early evening drink. Dine at the **Night Market** (see pp14–15) where you'll be spoiled for choice.

Day ❷
MORNING
From Jemaa el Fna (see pp12–13), dive into the **souks** (see pp16–17), then lunch at **Atay Café** (see p77).

AFTERNOON
Head to the nearby **Medersa Ben Youssef** (see pp28–9), then walk on to place du Moukef and catch a taxi to the **Majorelle Gardens** (see pp32–3). Admire the plants, then take a taxi to Guéliz for early evening drinks at the **Sky Bar** (see p56) before dining locally at **Al Fassia** (see p83).

Four Days in Marrakech

Day ❶
MORNING
Start with a walk around the **Koutoubia** (see pp20–21), before meandering over to the **Saadian Tombs** (see p68). Have lunch at **Café Clock** (see p71).

AFTERNOON
Head over to the **Badii Palace** (see pp30–31), then go by way of one of the rue Riad El Zitouns to **Jemaa el Fna** (see pp12–13). When you're ready for a break from bargaining, head to **La Mamounia Hotel** (see pp34–5) for a drink. Travel back to Jemaa el Fna (see pp12–13) to dine at the **Night Market** (see pp14–15).

TAXI

0 metres 500
0 yards 500

Atay Café

La Maison Arabe

Dar Moha

Place du Moukef

Medersa Ben Youssef

Maison de la Photographie

Dar Cherifa

MOUASSINE

SOUKS

Night Market

Jemaa el Fna

Rue Riad El Zitouns

Koutoubia

Dar Si Said Museum

La Mamounia Hotel

Saadian Tombs

Bahia Palace

Badii Palace

KASBAH

Café Clock

TAXI

Beldi Country Club 6 km (4 miles)

The souks are a warren of passageways filled with brightly coloured local wares and intriguing sights and smells.

The Majorelle Gardens make for a peaceful getaway from the rush of the Medina.

Day ❷

MORNING
Head out from Jemaa el Fna (see pp12–13) and stroll among the **souks** (see pp16–17) before heading to **Atay Café** (see p77) for lunch.

AFTERNOON
Visit the nearby **Medersa Ben Youssef** (see pp28–9) and wander the **Maison de la Photographie** (see p43). Make your way over to the Mouassine area, taking in **Dar Cherifa** (see p72), and dine at **Dar Moha** (see p77) or **La Maison Arabe** (see p77). Reservation needed.

Day ❸

MORNING
Take a taxi to the **Majorelle Gardens** (see pp32–3) and the neighbouring **Musée Yves Saint Laurent** (see pp32–3)

and then head to Guéliz to lunch at **MY Kechmara** (see p83) and explore the local boutiques.

AFTERNOON
Return to the Medina for a leisurely afternoon at a hammam (see pp46–7). Head to Guéliz for a drink at the **Grand Café de la Poste** (see p83).

Day ❹

MORNING
Return to the Kasbah area to visit the impressive **Bahia Palace** (see pp26–7) or the **Dar Si Said** Museum (see p68), then wrap up any souvenir shopping.

AFTERNOON
Take a taxi to the **Beldi Country Club** (see p53) for a late lunch, then spend the afternoon chilling beside the pool. Dine at **Comptoir Darna** (see p83).

Top 10 Marrakech Highlights

Minaret of the Koutoubia Mosque

 Marrakech Highlights

Marrakech may only be Morocco's third most important city after Rabat and Casablanca, but its fabulous palaces and palm groves exercise a powerful hold over tourists. Once a market town, located on the edge of nowhere, it remains an exotic port of call.

① Jemaa el Fna

This is a vast plaza at the heart of the Medina (the old walled city). The site of parades and executions in the past, it is the centre of modern city life (see pp12–13).

② The Night Market

By night, Jemaa el Fna turns into a circus, theatre and restaurant, with itinerant musicians and entertainers drawing crowds (see pp14–15).

③ The Souks

Laid out in the narrow streets north of Jemaa el Fna is an array of souks. Different areas specialize in their own wares, selling everything from carpets and slippers to ingredients for magic spells (see pp16–17).

④ Koutoubia Mosque

Marrakech's landmark monument has a tower that dominates the skyline for miles. It is closed to the public but it is an impressive sight nonetheless (see pp20–21).

⑤ City Walls and Gates

Marrakech's Medina is surrounded by several miles of reddish-pink dried-mud walls, punctuated by nearly 20 gates. Having proved ineffective against attackers throughout history, the walls are clearly more ornamental than functional these days (see pp24–5).

Bahia Palace

This vast palace complex, with its marble-paved courtyard, intricate ceilings and elaborate *zellij* tiling, is one of the most magnificent sights in Marrakech *(see pp26–7)*.

Medersa Ben Youssef

Behind a typically blank façade lies what is arguably the city's finest building. This ancient religious school features exquisite decoration *(see pp28–9)*.

Badii Palace

The ruins of this once fabled palace provide a picturesque setting for nesting storks, and a salutary warning from history against extravagance *(see pp30–31)*.

Majorelle Gardens

Jacques Majorelle, a French artist who came to Marrakech to recuperate, created this beautiful garden. It was later owned by French couturier Yves Saint-Laurent and is now open to the public *(see pp32–3)*.

La Mamounia Hotel

With luxurious suites and beautiful surrounding gardens, La Mamounia is a *grande dame* among hotels, and has welcomed the visiting rich and famous for almost a century *(see pp34–5)*.

TOP 10 ⭐ Jemaa el Fna

The Medina's central square means "Assembly of the Dead", a reference to a time when the heads of executed criminals would be displayed here on spikes. Although nothing so gruesome is on view today, the square is still populated with some extraordinary sights, including acrobats and colourfully costumed water sellers. Despite efforts to clean up and organize Jemaa el Fna with neat paving and ornamental barrows, the place remains endearingly chaotic.

1 Orange Juice Stalls

Sellers of freshly squeezed orange juice, with brightly painted barrows **(below)** are the first to appear on the square every morning.

2 Porters

With cars banned from crossing Jemaa el Fna, access to many of the hotels in the surrounding alleys is provided by the ubiquitous *carroser* (porter), who carries travellers' luggage on a wheelbarrow to their riad, guesthouse or hotel in return for a small tip.

3 Plants and Herb Stalls

Towards the back of the square, closest to the souks, are a number of small stalls selling plants and towering piles of herbs. Often overlooked, these stalls add a pop of greenery to Jemaa el Fna.

4 Acrobats

Acrobats and athletic young men **(left)** perform spectacular feats to entertain the audience and earn a few coins. Their repertoire usually includes cartwheels, somersaults and tottering pyramids.

5 Music

No matter the time of day or night, music is likely to be heard in the square. The most popular are the Gnawa musicians (see p14).

6 Herbalists

These stand as testimony to the Moroccan belief in natural remedies **(below)**. Compounds of ground roots, dried herbs and even desiccated animal parts are used for everything from curing colds to warding off the evil eye.

AN UNPLANNED MASTERPIECE

Jemaa el Fna square is considered to be a "Masterpiece of the Oral and Intangible Heritage of Humanity" by UNESCO. This is an international list that includes pieces of culture such as song cycles, theatrical traditions and sacred spaces. Inclusion in the list is intended to raise awareness and preserve something unique and irreplaceable; Jemaa el Fna certainly qualifies.

⑩ Water Sellers

Known to the locals as *gerrab*, these traditional water sellers **(left)** roam the square in colourful costumes and tassel-fringed hats, ringing copper bells to announce their arrival. The brass cups are exclusively for Muslims, while the white-metal cups are for everyone else. The water may upset visitors' stomachs.

⑦ Fortune-Tellers

Throughout the day, impossibly wrinkled elderly women squat beneath umbrellas with packs of tarot cards to read the fortunes of passersby.

⑨ Fruit and Nut Stalls

Near the orange juice stalls are vendors selling nuts and dry fruit by weight. Dates, figs and walnuts are a few Moroccan-grown products on offer here. Make sure to wash any purchases before consuming.

Café de France ⑧

There are several good places to sit and watch the incessant entertainment of the square over a coffee, but the raffish air of the Café de France **(right)** lends it an added appeal, making it a favourite with tourists and locals alike.

🔟 ⭐ The Night Market

Each evening as the sun goes down, dozens of open-air kitchens are set up on the eastern side of Jemaa el Fna. Serving areas are erected and tables and benches are put out to create one vast al fresco spot. Beneath a hanging cloud of smoke created by the crackling charcoal grills, locals and visitors alike tuck into a vast array of Moroccan cuisine. As the air fills with the aroma of spices, the square throngs with musicians, dancers and storytellers who draw in enthusiastic crowds.

1 Le Grand Balcon du Café Glacier
One of the best places to observe the spectacle of the Night Market is the atmospheric rooftop terrace of Le Grand Balcon du Café Glacier. Visit at sunset for superb views.

2 Khunjul Carts
In the evening, carts are set up in the front of the square with large brass kettles topped up with spicy hot tea. It is said to be a cure-all for any ailment – try a cup.

4 Promenade
Once dusk begins to fall, many visitors take a leisurely stroll through the square and along Rue Bab Agnaou. It's an ideal way to unwind and soak in the ambience.

5 Musicians
A smattering of musicians and groups of Gnawa (below) specialize in hypnotic rhythms and enchanting melodies which set the crowds swaying. Entranced listeners can linger in the square long after everyone else has gone home.

The lively Night Market

3 Shopping
Walk around to view what's on offer and when you see something you like, take a seat and just point to what you want. Prices are usually posted and everything is fairly inexpensive.

6 Storytellers
Gifted orators entertain with tales of Islamic heroes. Sessions are in Arabic and often end on a cliffhanger – the outcome is revealed the following night.

7 Street Food
The ingredients arrive fresh at the market each evening and a wide range of traditional dishes are cooked from scratch in front of you. Plates and utensils are often washed in water that isn't changed for much of the night, so it is best to get your food served on paper and eat with your fingers.

8 Local Flavours

Some of the most popular food offerings here are the varieties of *brochette* – grilled lamb and chicken – served along with bowls of soup, spicy merguez sausages, grilled fish and bowls of boiled chickpeas. Those feeling adventurous can try the stewed snails.

THE GNAWA

The Gnawa came to Morocco as enslaved people from sub-Saharan Africa. Over the centuries they have kept their culture alive through oral traditions, particularly music. Played on simple string instruments known as *gimbri*, their music is looping and repetitive, intended to induce an almost trance-like state in the dancers and the vocalists who often sing and chant along with the musicians. Gnawa music has made a great impact on the global music scene.

9 Entertainers

Wide-eyed onlookers surround a menagerie of illusionists, performers and fortune-tellers **(below)**. This is where the Moroccan belief in everyday magic is on full, authentic display.

10 Henna Painting

Ladies with piping bags full of henna paste paint hands and feet with intricate designs. Be aware, however, that the paste is often poor quality and can contain ingredients that may cause skin problems. The nearby Marrakech Henna Art Cafe *(see p71)* offers reputable products.

NEED TO KNOW

MAP J3 ▪ The Night Market sets up at sunset daily and runs until around midnight or later in the summer months.

Le Grand Balcon du Café Glacier: 0524 44 21 93; open 6am–10:30pm daily

▪ Although Marrakech has a very low crime rate, the crowds milling around Jemaa el Fna at night are perfect cover for pickpockets. Be careful with handbags, wallets and purchases.

▪ If you find the food stalls at the Night Market to be overwhelming, you can always opt for the relative familiarity of salads, pizza and pasta at Argana on the square instead.

TOP 10 ⭐ The Souks

Marrakech's earliest inhabitants made their living from trade, bartering with the Africans, and the Spaniards who came by sea. Luxuries like gold and ivory came from the south, while leather, metalwork and ceramics were sent north. Even today, trade continues to be the city's mainstay, with thousands of craftsmen making a living among the maze of souks that fill much of the northern half of the Medina. A trip to the souks is part history lesson, part endurance trial – testing how long travellers can keep their purse in their bag or their wallet in their pocket.

Souk des Tapis ①
This is the centre of the carpet trade in the city, with a variety of carpets **(right)** on sale here.

② Fondouks
The *fondouk* is an ancient hostelry for travelling merchants, built around a courtyard. These days, fondouks are workshops or shops.

③ Rahba Kedima
This open square is home to sellers **(above)** of traditional herbs and remedies. You may see other objects on display, but these are often just for show.

④ Souk El Kebir
Found straight on from rue Semmarine, this is the heart of the souks – a narrow alley that lurches from side to side and up and down. It is lined by tiny shops each overflowing with goods, especially leather.

⑤ Souk El Bab Salaam
This covered market serves the nearby Mellah quarter with everything from food to caged birds.

⑥ Souk des Teinturiers
Sheaves of freshly dyed wool are hung from ropes strung across one particular alleyway of the dyers' souk for a vibrant, colourful scene.

⑦ Souk Cherifia
A three-storey mini-market (see p76) within the souks, this is the place for edgier finds among a plethora of quirky, designer-owned boutiques.

The Souks

⑧ Souk des Ferronniers
The sound of hammering fills the air in this medieval part of the Medina where ironworkers **(above)** create furniture, lanterns and other items.

⑨ Rue Semmarine
The main route into the souks is via an arch just north of Jemaa el Fna and along this perpetually busy sun-dappled alley. Shop owners along Semmarine attempt to entice visitors with a miscellany of robes, kaftans, carpets and antiques.

⑩ Souk des Babouches
Every shop and stall here sells nothing but brightly coloured, soft-leather, pointy-toed slippers known as *babouches* **(left)**. Prices can vary widely between around 60 Dh and 400 Dh.

NEED TO KNOW

MAP K2 ■ Medina
■ Many of the shops and stalls in the souks are closed on Fridays

■ You can get lost in the souks. Alleys are narrow, winding and constantly branching, while landmarks are few. However, the area covered is small and you are never more than a few minutes' walk back to Jemaa el Fna. Watch out for the constant stream of scooters and bicycles in the narrow lanes.

■ Café Arabe *(see p77)*, near the Souk des Teinturiers, and Café des Epices *(see p77)* in the Rahba Kedima are both great places for some respite.

Guides
A guide to the souks can be really helpful, especially if you're short of time. Although the area is not too large, the souks are a warren and are confusing to navigate. When hiring a guide, check that they are licensed. You'll be led to various shops and stalls; be sure to bargain when buying goods.

Marrakech Souvenirs

Colourful Moroccan pottery featuring traditional patterns and glazes

1 Pottery

Each region of Morocco produces its own distinctive pottery. The Marrakech style is plain terracotta finished with colourful glazes, and ceramics from the Akkal factory would not look out of place in a cutting-edge design shop. Visit the big pottery souk outside Bab Ghemat, found to the southeast of the Medina, for a wide variety.

2 Carpets

Marrakech is famed for its carpets, made by the tribes of the south who each have their own patterns. Carpets come in all shapes and sizes. Most sold today, though beautiful, are quite modern and made from wool or a cotton and wool blend. Beware the salesmen's patter: buy a carpet if you like it, not because you have been told it is a good investment.

3 Candles

Candles are used to great effect in local riads, bars and restaurants. They are sold in all shapes, sizes and colours (and frequently scents), and some of the designs are highly inventive. You can find them in the souks and Guéliz boutiques, although the greatest selection is probably to be found in the industrial quarter outlets of Sidi Ghanem *(see p52)*.

4 Lanterns

There are two types of lanterns: those that are hung from the ceiling and those that sit on the floor. The former (known as *fanous*) are typically metal and come in elaborate shapes with intricate designs. The latter are made of skin and goats' hair and are usually very colourful. Look for them in the northern part of the souk.

Lantern

5 Marra-Kitsch

A trend among local designers involves taking Marrakech iconography and giving it a Pop Art twist. Hassan Hajjaj, known as the "Andy Warhol of Marrakech", makes *fanous* (lanterns) from sheets of tin printed with advertising logos.

6 Babouches

Babouches are Moroccan slippers, handmade from local leather, although increasingly the *babouches* found in the souks are made of a synthetic plastic that only looks like leather. In their most basic form they are pointy-toed and come in a variety of colours but are otherwise plain. It is becoming popular for boutiques and shops to customize their *babouches* with a silk trim, or even carve the leather with exquisite designs.

7 Jewellery

The local Amazigh jewellery is silver, chunky and heavy. There are a number of artisans in Marrakech, both local and foreign, that produce more modern designs as well. Look out for designer Joanna Bristow's brilliant creations in select hotel boutiques such as La Mamounia *(see pp34–5).*

A selection of Moroccan jewellery

8 Fashion

Marrakech has inspired countless foreign couturiers – from Yves Saint-Laurent to Tom Ford. However, the city has a vibrant fashion scene of its own, spearheaded by local designers including Artsi Ifrach, Norya Ayron and Noureddine Amir. Check out Souk Cherifia and other boutiques in Mouassine *(see p76),* and, in the New City, visit the excellent concept store 33 rue Majorelle *(see p82).*

An array of leather bags

9 Leather Bags

Marrakech is known for its leather. The animal hides are treated by hand in the tanneries *(see p74)* in the east of the Medina, and then dyed and shaped. Unsurprisingly, the shops of the souk are filled with leather goods, from purses and handbags to book bindings. Do plenty of window shopping before settling on an item.

10 Argan Oil

Argan oil *(see p95)* is an almost mystical substance to which all kinds of properties are attributed. Part of its mystique can be credited to the rarity of argan trees, which only grow in southwest Morocco. The oil is sold all over the souks. Quality oil has the consistency of olive oil and a neutral smell. Culinary oil should smell slightly nutty.

Extracting argan oil

🔟 ⭐ Koutoubia Mosque

Its minaret is the city's pre-eminent monument, towering above all else, and has always been the first visible sign of Marrakech for travellers approaching from afar. Its iconic status is fitting as the mosque is not only the city's main place of worship, but also one of its oldest buildings – it was built back in the 12th century, not long after Marrakech was founded. The designer of the Koutoubia minaret went on to create Tour Hassan in the Moroccan capital, Rabat, and the tower of the Giralda in Seville. As with nearly all mosques and shrines in Morocco, non-Muslims are not permitted to enter; however, the architecture can be appreciated from outside.

4 The Mosque Plan

The mosque's plan is rectangular in shape. The plain main entrance to the east leads to a vast prayer hall with eight bays and horse-shoe arches. North of the prayer hall is a 45-m (148-ft) wide courtyard with an ablution fountain and trees.

6 Minaret

The purpose of a minaret is to provide a high platform from which the muezzin can make the call to prayer five times a day. Rather than a simple staircase, the Koutoubia minaret (right) has a spiralling ramp wide enough for a horse to be ridden to the top.

1 Koubba Lalla Zohra

This white tomb (above) houses the body of Lalla Zohra, who spent her life in worship and is seen as a saint for her devotion.

5 Dar El Hajar

Two wells on the piazza allow visitors to view the buried remains of the Dar El Hajar (House of Stone), a fortress built by the Almoravids. It was destroyed when the Almohads captured the city in 1147 (see p38).

2 Mosque of the Booksellers

The Koutoubia was built in 1158. Its name means the *Mosque of the Booksellers*, which is a reference to a small market that once existed in the neighbourhood where worshippers could buy religious texts.

3 The Minaret Decoration

Originally the whole minaret was encased in tiles and stucco, but now only two bands of blue ceramic remain (right).

7 Prayer Times

Exact times of daily prayer change with the seasons, but they are observed five times a day, with sessions held pre-dawn, noon, late afternoon, sunset and late evening, as indicated by the muezzin, who sings the call to prayer. The most important prayers of the week are those on Friday at noon.

8 Ruins of the Almohad Mosque

Next to the Koutoubia are the remains of an earlier mosque, built c 1147. The bases of the prayer hall's columns, secured behind railings, are clearly visible. They were revealed during excavations by Moroccan archaeologists.

9 Koutoubia Gardens

South of the mosque is a garden **(above)** with a mix of palms and deciduous trees, topiary hedges and colourful roses.

HEIGHTS OF GOOD TASTE

The Koutoubia minaret's continued dominion over the skyline is owed to a piece of legislation imposed by the city's former French colonial rulers. They decreed that no building in the Medina should rise above the height of a palm tree, and that no building in the New City should rise above the height of the minaret. The ruling still holds today; the tower stands 70 m (230 ft) high, in proportions that obey the cannons of Almohad architecture (its height is five times its width).

NEED TO KNOW

MAP H4 ■ Ave Bab Jedid, Medina; open only during prayer times; closed to all non-Muslims

Koutoubia Gardens: entry is free to both Muslims and non-Muslims

■ Although access is denied to non-Muslims, one of the doors on the east wall is often open so visitors can peer through for a view of the prayer hall and its seemingly endless arcades of horseshoe arches.

■ Nearby, on Rue Lalla Fatima Zahara, is the restaurant Kabana. It offers good food and has a terrace with great views of the minaret.

10 Tomb of Youssef Ben Tachfine

Just north of the mosque, glimpsed through a locked gate, is a walled area containing the dilapidated mausoleum of Youssef Ben Tachfine (1009–1106) – tribal leader of the Almoravids and the man credited with the founding of Marrakech.

🔟 ⭐ City Walls and Gates

The city walls date from the 1120s when, under threat of attack from the Almohads of the south, the ruling Almoravid sultan, Ali Ben Youssef, decided to encircle his garrison town with fortifications. The walls he had built were up to 9 m (30 ft) high and formed a circuit of 10 km (6 miles), with some 200 towers and 20 gates. Even today, the walls remain largely unchanged.

NEED TO KNOW

Medina

Bab Debbagh: **MAP E5**; permission required to access the roof (not always open to visitors)

■ Walking a circuit around the walls can be unpleasant in the heat. It is better to visit the gates individually.

■ Make sure that you carry bottled water, as it can get hot.

■ As you tour the walls, look up to spot the storks that make their homes at the highest points. Note, too, the holes added for scaffolding, often raised to ensure the upkeep of the walls.

② Bab Berrima

Apart from serving as perimeter defences, walls and gates were also used to divide up the interior of the Medina. For instance, a wall separated the royal kasbah quarter from the city – Bab Berrima was one of the gates between these two distinct zones. This gate leads to the Medina's main souks.

③ Bab er Robb

This was the original southern city gate. The gatehouse building is now occupied by a pottery shop and all foot and car traffic passes through a modern breach in the old walls. The name translates as "Lord's Gate".

① Pisé

The walls **(above)** are built from a mixture of mud, straw and lime (known as pisé), which becomes as hard as brick on drying. The distinctive pinkish-red hue is a result of pigments in the earth.

City Walls and Gates

Previous pages Elaborate zellij tiling at the Dar Si Said Museum

⑥ Place des 7 Saints

Just outside the north side of the walls stand seven stone towers, each topped by a tree **(left)**. This giant ensemble pays homage to the seven patron saints *(see p75)* of Marrakech.

THE RED CITY

Marrakech's distinctive colouring comes from pigments in the local soil mixed to make the *pisé* from which the city's buildings were traditionally constructed. In the last century, this was threatened by new building materials such as concrete. The ruling French decreed that all new buildings be painted pink – a rule that continues to be enforced today with pleasing aesthetic results.

⑧ Bab Agnaou

The most beautiful of the city's gates, the "Gate of the Gnawa" **(left)** is the only stone-built one. It was erected during Almohad sultan Yacoub El Mansour's reign in the 12th century.

⑨ Bab Debbagh

This gate gives access to the tanneries, and when it is open, visitors can ascend an internal staircase to the gatehouse roof for sweeping city views.

④ Bab Doukkala

This massive gate, built by the Almoravids in the 12th century, now stands isolated from the walls due to 20th-century urban planning. The cavernous interior of the rooms are perfect for use as an event space.

⑦ Bab El Khemis

The northernmost gate, this is the most decorative, with a semicircle of stalactite mouldings over the entrance. A lively flea market **(below)** is held here on Thursdays from 8am to midday.

⑩ Dar El Haoura

West of the Agdal Gardens, this curious freestanding fortress used to be a garrison for cavalry and its horse ramp is intact to this day.

Bab Taghazout ⑤

Set at the northern edge of the Medina, the *bab* (gate) is near to Zaouia Sidi bel Abbès mosque, a complex centred around a shrine to one of the city's patron saints.

TOP 10 ⭐ Bahia Palace

The 19th-century Bahia Palace, literally meaning "Palace of the Favourite" or "Palace of the Beautiful", was constructed by two powerful grand viziers – Si Moussa, vizier of Sultan Sidi Mohammed ben Abderrahman, and his son Ba Ahmed, vizier of Moulay Abdelaziz. The older part, built by Si Moussa, has apartments arranged around a marble-paved courtyard and an open courtyard with two star-shaped pools. The newer part, built by Ba Ahmed, has luxurious apartments overlooking the courtyards. The palace covers 8 hectares (20 acres) and has 150 rooms, but only a small portion is open to the public.

① Courtyard of Honour

At the heart of the palace is a 1,500-sq-m (1,800-sq-yd) open-air courtyard **(above)**. Paved with Italian Carrara marble and *zellij* tilework, it has three fountains with bowls in the centre.

② Palace Layout

It may not seem apparent at first, but the palace's design is rather disjointed. This is because it was built in stages over many years. As you wander through the palace the influence of different architectural styles can be seen, from Andalucían near the entrance to Persian further back.

③ School and Mosque

Inside the palace is a Quranic school, which was also a mosque, where children living in the palace studied.

④ Andalucían Garden

Designed in Andalucían style, this garden **(below)** is split into four sections with a divider that breaks up the quadrants. Plants are arranged by size with smaller ones near the walkway and larger ones towards the back. In the middle of the garden is a fountain.

Large Riad ⑤

At the north end of the Courtyard of Honour is the Large Riad (right), which was the original palace of Si Moussa. It has a sleeping area and a private dining area. It is believed the Bahia Palace was the first building in North Africa to use stained glass for decor.

CREATING A MASTERPIECE

Ba Ahmed hired the best craftsmen in the kingdom to build and decorate the newer palace. It is decked out with highly prized materials, such as marble from Meknès, cedar from the Middle Atlas and tiles from Tetouan. Marble from Italy was also imported for its construction. Not surprisingly, French Army general Marshal Lyautey chose to live here during the Protectorate.

⑦ Petit Riad

This area features the Andalucían Garden and a small building, which resembles a traditional Medina house. Inside is the grand Council Chamber.

⑧ Doors and Windows

It's worth taking time to admire the doors and windows of the palace. The open-arched doors are either plaster carved or wood carved. The windows are a mixture of clear glass and stained glass, much of which was imported from Iraq.

⑩ Painted Wooden Ceilings

The intricately painted ceilings **(below)** are one of the palace's most unique features. Natural dyes from products, such as saffron and henna, were used to paint the ceilings in a style resembling carpet patterns.

⑥ Wives Bedrooms

According to Islamic law, all wives must be treated equally. This is why the four bedrooms, which were built for the sultan's wives, have the exact same proportions.

⑨ Council Chamber

This splendid room, featuring lots of stucco and wood work, was the council chamber for Ba Ahmed. It also has a fireplace inlaid with *zellij* tiles.

NEED TO KNOW

MAP K5 ◼ 5 rue Riad Zitoun El Jedid ◼ 0524 38 91 79

Open 9am–4:30pm daily

Adm: 70 Dh

◼ There is limited signage in the Bahia Palace, so visiting with a guide is recommended as they can regale you with stories of palace life and detail the complex's features.

◼ The site can be busy with large groups. Aim to arrive either at opening time or later in the day to avoid the crowds.

◼ Exploring this huge palace can work up an appetite. Grab a snack from one of the stalls on the northwest corner of nearby place des Ferblantiers.

TOP 10 ⭐ Medersa Ben Youssef

While not the oldest or most significant of Marrakech's monuments, the *medersa* is one of the city's most impressive buildings, and it allows entry to non-Muslims. Founded in the 14th century, it was restored and enlarged by the Saadian sultan Moulay Abdellah in around 1565. All the fine decorative detailing that characterizes the golden age of Moroccan architecture is evident in the *medersa*. The building has also had a brush with stardom as an Algerian Sufi retreat in the movie *Hideous Kinky*.

Main Courtyard ①
At the heart of the *medersa* is a light-filled courtyard **(right)** with arcades down two sides, a rectangular pool in the middle and a prayer hall. Every surface has some decoration.

② **Dar Bellarj**
To the north of the *medersa*'s entrance, Dar Bellarj is a former stork hospital (the name means "House of the Storks"). The building now houses a beautiful cultural centre with a programme of regularly changing exhibitions.

③ **Student Cells**
Arranged on two levels around the central courtyard are 130 tiny rooms, much like monks' cells **(above)**. Nearly 900 Muslim students studied here until the *medersa* fell out of use in the 1960s.

④ **Chrob ou Chouf Fountain**
A little north of the *medersa*, this handsome fountain is worth seeking out. With a big cedar lintel covered in calligraphy, it is from a time when it was a pious act to provide a public source of clean drinking water. Its name means "drink and look".

NEED TO KNOW

MAP K2 ▪ Place Ben Youssef, Medina
▪ 0524 44 18 93

Closed for renovation

Musée de Marrakech:
Place Ben Youssef; open: 9am–7pm daily (except religious holidays); Adm: 50 Dh; www.musee demarrakech.ma

▪ Musée de Marrakech has a courtyard that is used as an exhibition space. It features stained-glass windows, cedar archways, painted door panels and *zellij* (glazed tiles).

▪ A combined ticket of 60 Dh is available to visit the Musée de Marrakech and Koubba El Baddiyin.

5 Carved Stucco

The panels of intricately carved plaster that stretch above the tiling are decorated with inscriptions or geometric patterns **(left)** – depiction of humans or animals is prohibited by Islam.

BEN YOUSSEF MOSQUE

The *medersa*, in its earlier days, was part of the complex of the nearby Almoravid mosque, which was founded by Ali Ben Youssef during his reign (1106–42). For several centuries, this was the focal point of worship in the Medina, and, together with the *medersa*, it was considered a significant centre of the Islamic religion in Morocco.

8 Tiling

The lowest part of the courtyard wall is covered with *zellij* (glazed tiles) in an eight-pointed star motif **(below)**. Above this is a band of stylized Koranic text, interwoven with floral designs.

6 Prayer Hall

The elaborate prayer hall has an octagonal wooden-domed roof supported by marble columns **(below)**. The stucco features rare palm motifs and some calligraphy of Koranic texts. The room is well lit by gypsum windows.

7 The Role of the Medersa

A *medersa* was once a place for religious instruction – a theological college. The students who boarded here would have studied the Koran and discussed it with the institute's *fqih* or imam (learned religious figures).

9 Rue du Souk des Fassis

This winding alley to the *medersa's* east is lined by beautifully restored *fondouks* and old hostels. One is now a restaurant, Le Foundouk.

10 Ablutions Basin

Enter via a long corridor that leads to a square vestibule. On the left is a marble basin carved with floral motifs in the Andalusian style.

Badii Palace

It reputedly took armies of labourers and craftsmen 25 years to finish the Badii Palace. Completed in 1603, it was said to be among the most magnificent palaces ever constructed, with walls and ceilings encrusted with gold, and a pool with an island flanked by four sunken gardens. This grand folly survived for all of a century before yet another conquering sultan stripped the place bare – a process that took 12 years – and carted the riches to his new capital at Meknès. All that survives are the mudbrick ruins.

1 Mosque Minbar

An "annexe du palais" in the southeast corner displays the 12th-century *minbar* (pulpit) from Koutoubia Mosque. Intricately carved, this is a celebrated artwork of Moorish Spain.

2 Storks

The protrusions in the crumbling walls are well loved by the city storks that have made their nests here **(above)**. An old Amazigh belief has it that storks are actually transformed humans.

3 Khaysuran Pavilion

A pavilion on the north of the great court and once the palace harem, this space now serves as an exhibition hall, showing work by local and locally based foreign artists.

4 Rooftop Terrace

At the northeastern corner of the palace is the only intact tower with an internal staircase to the roof **(above)**. At the top, it is possible to get a sense of the immense size of the complex.

5 Basins and Gardens

The palace's central courtyard **(below)** is dominated by five basins and four sunken gardens planted with orange trees. The central basin has an island that comes alive every July for the Festival of Popular Arts. It is also used as a venue during the International Film Festival (see p42).

6 Sultan Ahmed El Mansour

The palace was built by El Mansour who became sultan after the Battle of Three Kings (1578), when the Moroccans defeated the Portuguese. Great wealth was accrued from the ransom of Portuguese captives and the riches were poured into the palace.

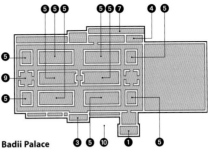

Badii Palace

7 The Gatehouse

The approach to the palace is found between twin high walls. On its completion, the gatehouse was carved with an inscription glorifying the palace. Now it is a ruin and the complex is entered through a breach in the crumbling walls.

8 A Sinister Omen

At a banquet to celebrate the palace's completion, a guest declared, "When it is demolished, it will make a fine ruin." The omen is now a reality.

9 Pavilion of 50 Columns

The ruins around the courtyard were probably summer houses. The Koubba El Khamsiniya **(left)** on the west side is named after the 50 pillars used to build it.

THE BATTLE OF THE THREE KINGS

In an attempt to steal the throne from his uncle, Abdel Malek, the Saadian sultan Abu Abdallah Mohammed II declared war along with King Sebastian of Portugal. All three died in the battle, fought in Ksar El Kebir, between Tangier and Fès. Malek was succeeded by his brother, Ahmed El Mansour, builder of the Badii Palace.

10 Underground Passages

Beside the annexe, a path leads down into the former stables and dungeon **(below)**. Though you can still enter, the chambers are only partially lit.

NEED TO KNOW

MAP K5 ■ Place des Ferblantiers, Medina

Open 9am–5pm daily

Adm: 70 Dh; plus 10 Dh for the *minbar* pavilion

■ This big site offers little shelter, so avoid visiting in the heat of the afternoon.

It is a good idea to bring bottled water with you.

■ In summer the palace is a venue for the Marrakech du Rire comedy festival.

■ Kosybar *(see p71)* is place des Ferblantiers' rooftop terrace. It offers the perfect spot for a bird's-eye view of the palace walls.

🔟 ⭐ Majorelle Gardens

These are the most famous of Marrakech's numerous gardens, and the legacy of an expatriate French painter, Jacques Majorelle, who considered himself a "gardenist". In 1923, he acquired land and set about creating a botanical sanctuary around his studio. Majorelle opened his gardens to the public in 1947 and they remained popular until his death 15 years later. They fell into disrepair until 1980, when they were rescued by fashion tycoons and partners Yves Saint-Laurent and Pierre Bergé.

1 Bassins and Fountains

The garden has a fountain and two large *bassins*, or pools **(above)**, the smaller of which is fed by a sloping channel. Next to the museum, a third pool is filled with a school of golden carp.

2 Boutique

In the northeast corner, a small boutique sells an interesting selection of quality local handicrafts including clothing, jewellery and miscellaneous leather products such as bags, sandals and beautifully bound notebooks. However, there is a notable paucity of information concerning Majorelle and his garden.

3 Majorelle Blue

The name Majorelle lives on in an electrifying shade of cobalt blue – known as "Majorelle blue" – that is widely used in the garden **(above)**.

4 Majorelle's Paintings

The museum's first room has a series of lithographs depicting various Atlas kasbahs. Some of Majorelle's most acclaimed works were the tourism posters that he created for Morocco.

5 Yves Saint-Laurent Memorial

The designer, who died in 2008, is remembered by a Roman column, which came from his Tangier home, placed on a red-ochre base **(left)**. His ashes were scattered around the gardens.

YVES SAINT-LAURENT (1936–2008)

French designer Yves Saint-Laurent first visited the city in 1962. By the end of the 1960s, he had bought his first house here. Later, he moved into a villa next to Majorelle Gardens, which he purchased and saved from being turned into an apartment complex. After his death a small memorial column was placed in the gardens. The Musée Yves Saint Laurent opened in late 2017, as a tribute to the designer.

7 Berber Museum

Jacques Majorelle's garden-villa-studio is now a museum dedicated to the Indigenous Amazigh people. More than 600 items illustrate aspects of their traditional culture (above).

8 Galerie Love

The "LOVE" posters Yves Saint-Laurent created using collage and sent yearly as New Year's greetings to friends and clients are exhibited here.

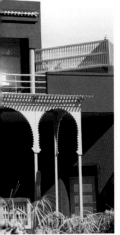

6 Jacques Majorelle

French artist Jacques Majorelle (1886–1962) came to Morocco in 1917 to recuperate from his heart problems and immediately saw the painterly potential of southern Morocco.

9 Musée Yves Saint Laurent

Situated next door to the Majorelle Gardens, this modern museum displays some of the French couturier's best-known looks. There is also an arts centre and an auditorium.

10 The Plants

A beautiful bamboo "forest" and an arid cactus garden with species from around the world share the garden (above). Most stunning of all are the flowering masses of red and purple bougainvillea.

NEED TO KNOW

MAP C4 ■ Rue Yves Saint-Laurent, Guéliz ■ 0524 31 30 47 ■ www. jardinmajorelle.com

Open 9am–6pm daily (last entry at 5:30pm)

Adm to gardens: 120 Dh; Berber Museum: 150 Dh

Musée Yves Saint Laurent: 0524 29 86 86; open 10am–6pm Thu–Tue; adm 100 Dh; www.museeysl marrakech.com

■ A relatively small site, Majorelle Gardens tend to get crowded

easily. Visit early in the morning or late in the afternoon to avoid the inevitable crowds and long queues.

■ A pleasant café located on site offers breakfast and lunch dishes as well as refreshing beverages.

TOP 10 ⭐ La Mamounia Hotel

One of the world's great old hotels, La Mamounia has been welcoming the rich and famous since opening its doors in 1923, with Winston Churchill being one of its most famous guests. Originally built as a palace in the 19th century for the crown prince of Morocco, it was turned into a hotel for the Moroccan railways by the French. Set within 7 hectares (17 acres) of delightful gardens, it is surrounded by the city's 12th-century red ochre ramparts.

The Rooms
Many of the rooms in this landmark hotel have been luxuriously renovated using wood and leather in warm Moroccan shades.

NEED TO KNOW

MAP H5 ■ Ave Bab Jedid, Medina ■ 0524 38 86 00 ■ www. mamounia.com

The Gardens: open 24 hours daily; non-guests allowed entry

■ Non-guests wishing to visit La Mamounia should dress smartly – people wearing flip flops, shorts and T-shirts are generally not allowed to enter.

■ The hotel has several restaurants and bars, but perhaps the most pleasurable of these is the lunch-time buffet that is served daily beside the swimming pool.

The grand courtyard of La Mamounia Hotel

Churchill's Paintings
Churchill would paint in the afternoon and was fond of Marrakech's extraordinary light. A couple of his paintings still hang in the hotel.

③ Guestbook
Scribbles by Sean Connery, Catherine Deneuve, Bill Clinton, Kate Winslet and Will Smith – La Mamounia's *livre d'or* must be among the starriest guestbooks.

④ The Man Who Knew Too Much
Several scenes of this 1956 Alfred Hitchcock thriller **(left)** featuring James Stewart and Doris Day were shot in the hotel, as well as other locations across the city.

The Suites 5

The most famous of the hotel's several grand suites is the one named after Winston Churchill **(right)**. The decoration is intended to evoke the politician's era and the suite contains several artifacts, including his pipe.

Winston Churchill 7

"This is a wonderful place, and the hotel one of the best I have ever used," were the words Churchill **(right)** used in a letter to Clementine, his wife, to describe the hotel and the city that he adored. Churchill *(see p45)* famously invited Franklin Roosevelt here during World War II.

Churchill Bar 10

One part of the hotel that was not altered during the recent makeover was this bar, named after the hotel's most famous guest. Cigar smoking is permitted, but shorts and T-shirts are not allowed.

The Architects 8

The original architects of La Mamounia blended Art Deco with traditional Moroccan motifs. In 1986, renovations were carried out by the designers of Morocco's royal palaces, further changing the character of the building.

The Gardens 6

The acres of formal European-style gardens were laid out for the prince and predate the construction of the hotel. Well-manicured paths lead between ponds and flowerbeds to a central pavilion **(right)**.

Majorelle Ceiling 9

Winston Churchill met fellow painter Jacques Majorelle in the winter of 1946 during one of his many stays at La Mamounia. The politician persuaded the hotel's management to commission a mural by Majorelle **(left)**, which you can now see on the ceiling of the extended lobby. Today, the Frenchman is best known for his creative master-piece, the Majorelle Gardens *(see pp32–3)*.

The Top 10
of Everything

**The serene, elaborately designed
inner courtyard of Riad Kniza**

Moments in History

1 Founding of Marrakech

The Almoravids, the most powerful Amazigh tribe, founded the military outpost of Marra Kouch in 1062, giving them control of the Saharan trade routes.

Koutoubia Mosque, Marrakech

2 The Almohads Take Marrakech

The Almohads lay siege to Marrakech in the year 1147 and control of the city changed hands. Their impressive monuments, including the Koutoubia Mosque, still dominate Marrakech.

Sultan Moulay Hassan

3 Decline Under the Merenids

Emerging from eastern Morocco, the Merenids took the city from the weakening Almohads in 1269. During their rule, Marrakech was sidelined and reduced to a provincial outpost after they chose the northerly city of Fès as their power base.

4 The Saadians

Prosperity returned to Marrakech under the Saadians, who overthrew the Merenids in 1549. This first Arab dynasty expanded their territory across the Western Sahara and over to Mali and Mauritania.

5 Moulay Ismail

The Saadians were swept aside by the Alaouites in 1668. Their second ruler, Moulay Ismail, was noted as much for his cruelty as for his diplomacy skills. He reigned for 55 years. The Alaouite dynasty still rules Morocco today.

6 French Rule

The lynching of Europeans in Casablanca gave France an excuse to implement its territorial ambitions. The consequent March 1912 Treaty of Fès made Morocco France's protectorate. In this period, a whole *nouvelle ville* (new city) was built outside the walls of the Medina.

Tribal warlord Thami El Glaoui

7 The Lord of the Atlas

The French enlisted tribal warlord Thami El Glaoui to rule southern Morocco from 1918 to 1955. The self-styled "Lord of the Atlas" was known for his cruelty and ruled the city with an iron fist.

8 Return of the King

November 1955 marked the return of exiled Sultan Mohammed V who was crowned king, with Morocco gaining independence a year later.

9 Marrakech Goes Global

During the 1960s, new policies on hotel ownership and development propelled the city towards a tourism boom, attracting travellers from all walks of life, including hippies, rock stars, journalists and celebrities. In 1985, the old town was designated a UNESCO World Heritage Site.

10 Reaching New Heights

In 2001, King Mohammed VI (grandson of Mohammed V) launched a national tourism strategy, which included plans for heavy investment and sustainable development. Marrakech made the most of the opportunities this offered and was one of the success stories welcoming a record three million tourists in 2019. A year later, the city hit another milestone when its population reached one million.

TOP 10 MARRAKECH READS

1 In Morocco (1920)
A visit to Morocco and Marrakech in 1917 inspired novelist Edith Wharton to try her hand at travel writing.

2 Morocco That Was (1921)
An entertaining account (especially of the Moroccan royalty) by *Times* correspondent Walter Harris.

3 A Year in Marrakech (1953)
Peter Mayne's engaging journal captures the essence of a city little-changed since medieval times.

4 Lords of the Atlas (1966)
A history of the colourful El Glaoui era by Gavin Maxwell.

5 A Street in Marrakech (1975)
This memoir by American Elizabeth Warnock tells of the struggles she and her family faced while living in Marrakech during the 1970s.

6 The Tangier Diaries (1997)
An account by John Hopkins of 1950s Tangier, featuring drug-fuelled forays to Marrakech.

7 Hideous Kinky (1998)
Esther Freud's autobiographical account of a dysfunctional 1970s childhood in Marrakech.

8 Marrakech: The Red City (2003)
A collection of writings on Marrakech down the ages from writers such as George Orwell and Edith Wharton.

9 Welcome to Paradise (2003)
Mahi Binebine tells the story of would-be migrants to Europe, setting off from a café on Jemaa el Fna.

10 The Last Storytellers: Tales from the Heart of Morocco (2011)
BBC journalist Richard Hamilton relates tales heard from the professional storytellers of Jemaa el Fna.

Author Peter Mayne

Moroccan Architecture

1 Stucco Plaster
A decorative element of Moroccan architecture, carved plaster can cover entire walls in fantastic design. The work is executed by craftsmen while the plaster is still damp – the patterns are sketched onto the surface, then gouged out with hammer and chisel.

2 Pigeonholes
The numerous pigeonholes peppering the walls in the city are, in reality, remnants of wooden scaffolding used to erect walls.

3 Tadelakt Plaster
This technique was initially used in bathhouses to counter the heat and moisture. Walls are treated with a limestone plaster, which, once set, is polished with flat stones, then glazed with egg whites and polished again with local black soap made from olives. The finished surface looks akin to soft leather.

4 Courtyards
A distinctive feature of Islamic architecture is its focus on the interior rather than the exterior, which is generally windowless. Courtyards serve as air-wells into which the cool night air sinks. They also allow women to enjoy the outdoors without having to cover up.

Typical Moroccan courtyard

Carved woodwork on a door

5 Carved Woodwork
Although some of the same designs are used to decorate both plaster and wood, the latter often has inscriptions in Arabic, the sacred language in which the Koran was revealed to the Prophet Mohammed. The inscriptions are of a religious nature and invariably praise the glory of Allah. They are both decorative and informative.

6 Fountains
Fountains and basins are required for ritual ablutions before prayers. With such an arid climate, the provision of drinking water is also seen as a charitable act.

7 Square Minarets

The square design of Moroccan minarets can be traced to the Umayyad rulers of Islamic Spain, who were of Syrian origin. Syrians are almost unique in the Middle East for their square minarets, probably influenced by the church towers built by Syrian Christians.

8 Pisé

The basic building material used in Morocco, *pisé* is wet earth that is mixed with straw and gravel pounded between two parallel boards and strengthened by lime. If it is not made well, the mixture can cause the structure to crumble in the rain – southern Morocco is littered with semi-melted buildings.

Colourful *zellij* terracotta tiles

9 Zellij Tiling

One of the most striking features of Moroccan architecture is its use of small, multicoloured tiles laid in complex geometric patterns. This is known as the *zellij* technique, where tiles are created as large squares and then hand-cut into smaller shapes. Conventional shapes and sizes are typically used, though there are as many as 360 different types of pieces.

10 Horseshoe Arches

Properly known as *outrepassé* arches, these are where the arch curves back inwards after its widest point, to give an effect like a keyhole or horseshoe. This design is most commonly associated with Moorish Spain and North Africa.

TOP 10 HISTORIC BUILDINGS

Bab Agnaou gate

1 Bab Agnaou
This gate (*see p25*) into the kasbah quarter is an impressive keyhole arch.

2 Koutoubia Mosque
Marrakech's biggest and tallest minaret (*see pp20–21*) can be found here.

3 Badii Palace
Its *pisé* walls (*see pp30–31*) are in an advanced state of dilapidation with clearly visible "pigeonholes".

4 Bahia Palace
This 19th-century palace (*see pp26–7*) features a riot of *zellij* work.

5 Medersa Ben Youssef
This structure (*see pp28–9*) displays an array of decorative elements, including fine *zellij* work, superbly carved stucco and woodwork.

6 Tin Mal Mosque
Some rare, surviving carved plasterwork dating to the early Almohad dynasty adorns the interiors of this mosque (*see p94*).

7 Koubba El Badiyin
The earliest example of Islamic architecture (*see p75*) in Marrakech with beautifully carved plasterwork seen nowhere else in Morocco.

8 Dar Cherifa
Home to a busy cultural centre, this townhouse (*see p72*) is an example of a wealthy courtyard with some extraordinary carved woodwork.

9 Dar El Bacha
Enough dazzling, multicoloured, polychromically patterned *zellij* tiling to make your head spin.

10 Dar Si Said Museum
Visit this museum (*see p68*) for an insight into architectural techniques and decoration.

⭐🔟 Arts and Culture

Modern art at David Bloch Gallery

① David Bloch Gallery
MAP B5 ■ 8 bis rue des Vieux Marrakchis, Guéliz ■ 0524 45 75 95 ■ Open 11am–6pm Tue–Sat ■ www.davidblochgallery.com

To see the new face of Marrakech art, visit this stylish gallery specializing in contemporary Moroccan art and graffiti.

② Musée Douiria de Mouassine
MAP J2 ■ 4–5 derb el Hammam, Mouassine ■ 0524 37 77 92 ■ Open 10am–6pm Sat–Thu ■ Adm ■ www.museedemouassine.com

A former home of a 16th-century Saadian noble, this is one of the city's most delightful museums, with the family's living quarters carefully restored. There are great views from the small rooftop café (see p74).

③ Musée d'Art et de Culture de Marrakech (MACMA)
MAP C5 ■ 61 rue de Yougoslavie, Guéliz ■ 0700 24 25 72 ■ Open 10am–7pm Mon–Sat ■ www.museemacma.com

This elegant gallery displays works by artists who fell in love with Marrakech including Jacques Majorelle, Eugène Delacroix and Raoul Dufy. Temporary exhibitions highlight Moroccan artists.

④ Galerie 127
MAP B5 ■ 127 ave Mohammed V, Guéliz ■ 0524 43 26 67 ■ Open 3–7pm Thu–Sat ■ www.galerie127.com

The first gallery in North Africa devoted to photography, this white-walled space in Guéliz exhibits many big names.

⑤ Marrakech International Film Festival
www.festivalmarrakech.info

Sponsored by movie fan King Mohammed VI, the festival was launched in 2001 and is held in December. A number of stars have graced the red carpet, including Martin Scorsese and Sean Connery.

⑥ Dar Cherifa
This 16th-century townhouse is a cultural centre that hosts regular exhibitions, with Gnawa musicians (see p15) often performing on opening nights. The small library offers art and heritage books to browse while enjoying tea or coffee (see p72).

Interior of Dar Cherifa

⑦ Galerie SINIYA28
MAP B5 ■ 28 rue Tarik Ibn Ziad ■ 0524 43 43 53 ■ Open 10:30am–1pm & 2:30–7pm Mon–Sat ■ www.galeriesiniya28.com

The exhibits at this modern art gallery focus on representing both Moroccan and international up-and-coming artists.

Maison de la Photographie

⑧ Maison de la Photographie

MAP K2 ▪ 46 rue Souk Ahal Fassi, Medina ▪ 0524 38 57 21 ▪ Open 9:30am–7pm daily ▪ www.maison delaphotographie.ma

This is a small museum dedicated to photographs taken by travellers to Morocco from the late 19th century to the 1960s. It occupies a beautiful old courtyard house which is not far from the Medersa Ben Youssef. The rooftop café is a refreshing place to stop for a glass of mint tea and take in the view.

⑨ Marrakech Street Art

Throughout Marrakech you will see graffiti art on the walls. Some are remnants from the Marrakech Biennale, a former arts festival, while others have been commissioned over the years. Adorning a full wall directly across from the Marrakech train station is a large black-and-white image of an older local man by German artist Hendrik Beikirch.

⑩ Marrakech National Festival of Popular Arts

Troupes from all over Morocco perform at this celebration of Amazigh music and dance held every year in June or July. Don't miss *fantasia*, an energetic charge of Amazigh horsemen outside the ramparts near the Bab El Jedid.

TOP 10 MOROCCAN CULTURAL FIGURES

1 Tahar Ben Jelloun
Morocco's best-known French-based writer won the French Prix Goncourt in 1987 for his novel *The Sacred Night*.

2 Mahi Binebine
This Marrakech-based artist authored the excellent *Welcome to Paradise*.

3 Hassan Hajjaj
The graphic artist behind the T-shirts worn by the staff at London's famous Moroccan restaurant, Momo.

4 Laïla Marrakchi
This Casablanca-born film-maker's debut feature, *Marock*, caused a scandal on its release in 2006.

5 Farid Belkahia
Famous for painting on lamb-skin canvases, Belkahia, one of Morocco's most influential artists, died in 2014.

6 Jamel Debbouze
Known for his roles in *Amélie* and *Days of Glory*, this French-Moroccan actor also runs the Marrakech du Rire comedy festival.

7 Elie Mouyal
This well-known architect is hugely popular among celebrities looking for a suitably fancy residence.

8 Master Musicians of Jajouka
International fame came upon this musical ensemble from a north Moroccan village, courtesy of the Rolling Stones.

9 Leila Abouzeid
The first female Moroccan author to have her work translated into English.

10 Hassan Hakmoun
Based in New York, this Moroccan trance specialist performed on Jemaa el Fna as a child.

Hassan Hakmoun

TOP10 Hammams and Spas

1 Heritage Spa
MAP H2 ▪ 40 Arset Aouzal, Bab Doukkala, Medina ▪ 0524 38 43 33 ▪ Open 10am–8pm daily ▪ Credit cards accepted ▪ www.heritagespamarrakech.com

A modern spa with a wide variety of treatments and packages at reasonable prices, the Heritage is extremely friendly and has English-speaking staff. It is an ideal option if you have never experienced a *hammam* before.

Products used in spa treatments

2 Les Bains de Marrakech
MAP J6 ▪ 2 derb Sedra, Mechouar Bab Agnaou, Kasbah ▪ 0524 38 64 19 ▪ Open 9am–7pm daily ▪ Credit cards accepted ▪ www.lesbainsdemarrakech.com

This spa provides a dazzling selection of treatments such as water massage, shiatsu massage and the intriguingly named "four-handed massage". Unusually, the *hammam* offers small, mixed steam-bath cubicles (swimsuits are compulsory). The adjacent Riad Mehdi is there to quench your thirst after all the exertion.

Les Bains de Marrakech

3 Hammam Ziani
MAP K4 ▪ Rue Riad Zitoun el Jedid, Medina ▪ 0662 71 55 71 ▪ Open 9am–10pm daily

Located near the Bahia Palace, this *hammam* offers all the facilities that you would expect (scrub, soak, steam and pummel) in surroundings that are significantly cleaner than those found in other medina bathhouses.

4 Hammam de la Rose
MAP J2 ▪ 130 Dar El Bacha, Medina ▪ 0524 44 47 69 ▪ Open 10am–8pm daily ▪ AmEx, MC, V accepted ▪ www.hammamdelarose.com

Smarter than the public *hammams* but not as over the top as some full-service spas, the Hammam de la Rose is a good mid-range option for Moroccan-style luxury that doesn't break the bank. Reasonably priced packages include *hammam* treatments with body scrubs followed by massages.

5 La Maison Arabe
The *hammams* housed in larger riads and hotels are often restricted to guests, but not at La Maison Arabe *(see p112)*. Book yourself in for a vigorous *gommage* (rubdown) with a *kissa* (loofah mitten) and follow it up with a soothing back, face, or foot massage.

6 Hammam El Bacha
MAP H3 ▪ 20 rue Fatima Zohra, Medina ▪ Open: men 7am–1pm daily; women 1–9pm daily ▪ No credit cards

One of the city's most historic *hammams*, this spot is thronged by tourists as well as the locals. The staff of the Dar El Bacha, just across the road, were its first patrons. The highlight is an impressive 6-m (20-ft) cupola in the steam room.

Previous pages Atmospheric interiors of Hammam de la Rose

The opulent basement *hammam* at La Sultana

(7) La Sultana

A five-star hotel (*see p112*) next to the Saadian Tombs, La Sultana has a beautiful basement spa complete with a star-domed marble Jacuzzi, a *hammam*, balneotherapy baths, open-air massage cabins and a solarium. Packages include massages, aroma-therapy and seaweed treatments. It gets busy so book well in advance.

(8) Farnatchi Spa

The day spa in Riad Farnatchi (*see p112*) is exquisitely designed, with private marble *hammams* featuring vaulted ceilings and a courtyard café for lunch. Visitors can even hire the whole spa for the day. Combine a body scrub treatment with an aromatic mask and finish with a beldi massage using black soap.

(9) Royal Mansour

As ornate and opulent as the five-star hotel (*see p112*) itself, the Royal Mansour is exqui-site. The white wrought-iron atrium brings to mind a giant bird enclo-sure – complete with the

sound of birdsong. Sprawling across three floors, the spa also includes a large indoor swimming pool as well as a fitness centre.

(10) Riad Noir d'Ivoire

This hip riad (*see p115*) includes Coco's Spa, offering a *hammam* and spa treatments such as an hour-long massage in front of a fire. Other treatments include hot-stone massages, reflexology and Coco's signature massage combining Moroccan and Thai methods.

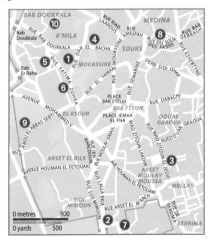

Riads

Shaded dining areas and colourful cushions on the roof terrace at Riad Kniza

1 Riad Kniza
A 200-year-old town house that has been beautifully restored by a local antiques dealer, Riad Kniza *(see p114)* showcases the best of Moroccan arts and crafts throughout its rooms and public spaces. Attentive service adds to the sensation that you're staying in a palace.

2 Riad Kheirredine
Its blend of traditional Amazigh decor and 21st-century gadgetry, including the Bluetooth music systems, makes this riad *(see p114)* stylish and smart. But what sets it apart is the exemplary service, including free bottles of mineral water and pastries, as well as pre-paid mobile phones for its guests.

3 Riad AnaYela
A captivating riad *(see p114)* with a compelling story: the name ("I am Yela") comes from the first words of a manuscript that was found in a hidden room during the riad's reconstruction, telling a tale of forbidden love. Small and lavishly appointed, it offers a special stay.

4 Riad Farnatchi
The intimate yet deluxe Farnatchi *(see p112)* has a design that is a playful update of the local aesthetic. Luxurious suites feature sunken baths and stylish private terraces offering gorgeous panoramic views. Almost like mini-riads, some suites have marble fountains and elaborate fireplaces.

Courtyard pool at Riad Farnatchi

Riad Noir d'Ivoire

Combining playfulness and elegance, this is a good option *(see p115)* for fashionistas. It has sumptuous photoshoot-friendly decor, a backlit bar serving a range of delicious cocktails, a relaxing *hammam* and its own boutique.

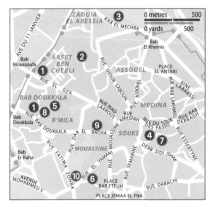

6 Dar Attajmil

This tiny riad *(see p114)* with four rooms and a roof terrace overlooks a small courtyard filled with banana trees. The rooms here have dark-wood ceilings and *tadelakt* bathrooms *(see p40)*. Its restaurant offers organic food from the owners' farm near Essaouira. The proprietors also run a two-bedroom mini-riad up the road and can easily arrange cookery classes and airport transfers.

7 Tchaikana

Reasonably priced, this riad *(see p117)* has two suites, two big double rooms and one smaller double room. The decor in each room is beautiful and highlights the "African" in North African. The rooms are set around a large central courtyard that is used for breakfasts and candlelit dinners. Don't miss the riad's celebrated crêpes at breakfast.

8 Riad Al Massarah

While this Anglo-French-owned riad *(see p114) is* run with an environmental and social conscience, there has been no skimping on the standard of its amenities, luxuries or the quality of its service.

9 Riad Adore

Tucked into the Dar el Bacha neighbourhood of the Medina, this riad *(see p114)* houses ten unique rooms. The simple, modern Moroccan design is accented with traditional *zellij* tiling and iron work. Be sure to enjoy the relaxing library or indulge in a treatment at the spa located on the roof terrace.

Cosy interiors of El Fenn

10 El Fenn

Founded by Vanessa Branson, El Fenn *(see p112)* is a sort of super-riad with its four courtyards, three pools, bar, restaurant, *hammam*, library, cinema screening room and collection of modern art including Branson's own work – all shared by just 28 rooms and 56 guests. The roof terrace offers spectacular views of the Atlas Mountains.

🔟 Parks and Gardens

Majorelle Gardens viewpoint

1 Majorelle Gardens

Formerly owned by Yves Saint-Laurent *(see p44)*, the gardens *(see pp32–3)* were first created by expatriate French artist Jacques Majorelle. Though small, they are quite lovely, with bamboo groves, cacti, palms, and pools floating with water lilies. The artist's former studio is now a museum, painted a searing blue that is known as "Majorelle blue".

2 Mamounia Gardens

Landscaped with flowerbeds and olive and citrus groves, these gardens predate La Mamounia Hotel *(see pp34–5)*. The Arset El Mamoun were established in the 18th century by Prince Moulay Mamoun, laid out around a central pavilion that served as a royal residence.

3 Le Jardin Secret

MAP J2 ▪ 121 rue Mouassine, Medina ▪ 0524 39 00 40 ▪ Open Feb, Mar & Oct: 9:30am–6:30pm daily; Apr–Sep: 9:30am–7:30pm daily; Nov–Jan: 9:30am–6pm daily ▪ Adm ▪ www.lejardinsecretmarrakech.com

Opened to the public in 2016, this large courtyard garden is in the middle of the Medina. Pleasant rather than spectacular, it is a fine place to relax with a mint tea.

4 Menara Gardens

MAP B7 ▪ Ave de la Menara, Hivernage ▪ 0524 43 95 80 ▪ Open 9am–5pm daily ▪ www.jardin-menara.com

Laid out in the 12th century, the Menara Gardens, with their orchard, pool and pavilion, epitomize a typical Islamic garden. The large pool is overlooked by a green-tile-roofed pavilion.

Menara Gardens pavilion

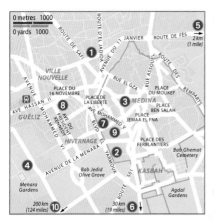

8 Jnane El Harti

Pretty and often quiet, this neatly planted green space (see p80) is beloved by locals, with its proximity to places of work making it a favourite lunchtime hangout. Come evening, visitors will spot young couples looking for a few private moments away from the prying eyes of families and relatives.

9 Koutoubia Gardens

On the south side of the landmark mosque (see p21), these formal gardens have stone pathways lined with flowerbeds and topiary hedges. The roses seem impervious to the heat and appear to be in bloom throughout the year.

5 Musée de la Palmeraie

MAP F4 ■ Dar Tounsi, route de Fes ■ 0628 03 10 39 ■ Open 9am–6pm daily ■ www.benchaabane.com/musee_palmeraie

This harmonious blend of nature and culture is set in a vast palm oasis (the Palmeraie) on the edge of town. The museum exhibits contemporary Moroccan art. There are also several fine thematic gardens inhabited by tortoises, turtles and frogs.

6 Anima Garden

MAP C1 ■ Douar Sbiti, Route d'Ourika ■ 0524 48 20 22 ■ Open 9am–6pm daily ■ Adm ■ www.anima-garden.com

Artist André Heller's Anima Garden features local flowers and trees interspersed with funky sculpture elements. There is an on-site café, which is a great place to sit with a drink and soak up the views. Tickets can be purchased online and a shuttle service from the city is available.

Dar al Hossoun gardens

7 Cyber Parc Arsat Moulay Abdeslem

MAP G3 ■ Ave Mohammed V ■ Open 7:30am–6:30pm daily

This public garden, between avenue Mohammed V and the walls of the Medina, has been given a makeover. The lawns, divided by palm-shaded pathways, are a favourite lunch spot. The park also has free Wi-Fi hot spots.

10 Dar al Hossoun

Taroudant ■ 0665 02 82 74 ■ www.alhossoun.com

The desert gardens at Hossoun, a guesthouse in the town of Taroudant in southern Morocco, contain more than 900 different species of plants. The gardens can be booked for private tours.

Off the Beaten Track

① Jarjeer Donkey Sanctuary

MAP C1 ■ Rue d'Amizmiz ■ www.jarjeer.org

Jarjeer is a retirement home, care centre and orphanage for mules and donkeys in a beautiful valley in the foothills of the Atlas Mountains. There is a coffee shop here and purchases help to support the sanctuary. It is 24 km (15 miles) from Marrakech on the Route d'Amizmiz, near Oumnass village.

② Sidi Ghanem

MAP C1 ■ 219 Quartier Industriel Sidi Ghanem

Anyone serious about shopping for homeware and interior decor items (candles, pottery, linen, furniture) should head to this industrial estate on the northern fringes of town, which has become the city's "design district". It is home to more than a dozen fantastic shops (start with Maison Fenyadi) and has a scattering of cafés and restaurants for between-purchase sustenance.

Crockery at Maison Fenyadi

③ Horse Trekking

www.naturallymorocco.co.uk

An excellent way of getting off the beaten track is to head out of the city into the surrounding desert on horseback. There are plenty of companies in and around Marrakech that provide horses, equipment and guides. The length of rides available varies from a few hours to a whole week, and there are a number of treks on offer, including coastal, desert and mountain rides.

Miâara Jewish Cemetery

④ Miâara Jewish Cemetery

MAP L5 ■ Ave Taoulat El Miara

In the early 20th century there were 36,000 Jews living in Marrakech, but now there are only maybe a couple of hundred. Evidence of this lost populace can be seen at this immense, sprawling, 200-year-old walled cemetery in the little-visited southeast corner of the Medina.

⑤ La Pause

MAP C1 ■ Douar Lmih Laroussiene, Agafay ■ www.lapause-marrakech.com

Another option for getting out of the city, this lodge is set in the arid Agafay valley about 40 minutes southwest of Marrakech. It is a chic eco-resort offering a choice of accommodation – nomad tents strewn with Amazigh rugs and cushions, or partially open huts made of *pisé*. There are plenty of activities on offer, including swimming, horse trekking, *pétanque* and golf.

6 Take a Day Trip

Head out of the city in any direction to lose the crowds. There are a number of worthwhile day trips such as the barrage at Lalla Takerkoust *(see p63)*, where you can swim while enjoying superb mountain views.

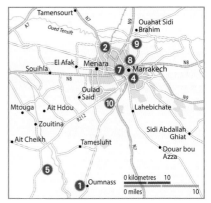

7 Marché Central

MAP C4 ■ Rue Ibn Toumert

Set away from the Medina, just east of place du 16 Novembre and behind the modern shopping centre, this is where locals and the city's expats do their shopping. Mixed in with the food stalls is a handful of craft shops where both quality and price tend to be better than the souks.

8 Souk El Khemis

MAP D4 ■ Bab el Khemis

Entrepreneurs renovating riads scout this flea market just north of the Medina walls for unusual finds, including carved doors and other bits of recycled handiwork.

9 Palmeraie Palace

This palm grove north of the city is the favoured retreat of the rich.

One of the pools at Palmeraie Palace

Among the secluded villas are also several upmarket hotels, including the Palmeraie – one of North Africa's leading golf resorts. Guests can play its 27-hole course and there are numerous restaurants and bars as well as a free kids' club *(see p117)*.

10 Beldi Country Club

MAP C1 ■ Route de Barrage
■ www.beldicountryclub.com

Escape the dust and chaos of the Medina to this chic rural retreat just beyond the city centre. Among shaded olive groves and rose gardens are restaurants, pools, a tennis court and a spa. Visitors can book cooking and pottery lessons, and the site includes a luxurious hotel for overnight stays.

🔟 Children's Attractions

Local performers dressed in vibrant clothes at Jemaa el Fna

1 Jemaa el Fna

With jugglers, acrobats and musicians, Jemaa el Fna *(see pp12–13)* will definitely capture children's imaginations. Make sure kids have adequate protection from the heat during the day, especially during the summer months when temperatures can top 40° C (104° F) .

2 Horse Riding
Royal Club Equestre, Route du Barrage (opposite Oasiria) ▪ 0524 38 18 49

Ponies and horses can be ridden at the Palmeraie Palace *(see p117)*. The Royal Club Equestre also has horses and ponies available to hire for both adults and children under ten years of age (rides of around 15 minutes each are offered).

3 Swimming

The Palmeraie Palace *(see p117)* allows non-guests the use of its swimming pool for a fee. It also has a popular children's play area.

4 Jnane El Harti

This public park *(see p80)* is a good place for a picnic and for children to let off some steam. Explore the paths, find huge cacti and admire the giant palm trees.

5 Child-Friendly Eating

Parents of fussy eaters might be glad of Le Catanzaro *(see p83)*, an Italian restaurant located in Guéliz that makes mini pizzas from a wood-fired oven for children, as well as classic pasta dishes and generous desserts, including giant pavlovas. Alternatively, there are ubiquitous McDonald's outlets nearby for a quick bite.

6 Kawkab Jeux
MAP C5 ▪ **1 rue Imam Shafi, Kawkab Centre, Hivernage** ▪ 0524 43 89 29 ▪ Open 10:30am–11pm daily

South of the Jnane El Harti, next to the Royal Tennis Club, this bright coffee shop and ice-cream parlour also has an indoor and outdoor play area. Kids can play table football, table tennis and video games.

Seahorse rocker at Kawkab Jeux

7 Palooza Park

koudiate Laabid, Route de Casablanca ▪ Opening times vary ▪ www.paloozaland.com

This dinosaur-themed park features more than a dozen exciting rides along with a swimming pool and restaurants. There are also many shows that provide entertainment for children.

8 Oasiria

Km 4, Route d'Amizmiz ▪ 0524 38 04 38 ▪ Open 10am–6pm daily; closed late Oct–late Mar ▪ Adm ▪ www.oasiria.com

South of the city, this large waterpark features a wave pool, a covered and heated pool, an artificial river, beach and many restaurants. A free shuttle runs every 45 minutes from 9:30am from Jemaa el Fna and Guéliz.

Artificial river, Oasiria

9 Child-Friendly Accommodation

Coralia Club Palmariva, Km 6, Route de Fès ▪ 0672 73 97 78

Guests travelling with kids can opt for one of the larger hotels (*see p113*) instead of the smaller riads. With a pool, playground, and an activity centre, the Coralia Club Palmariva is child-friendly.

10 Creative Interactions

MAP C4 ▪ Apt 47, Ave Hassan II Immueble El Khalil, Gueliz ▪ 0611 03 05 05 ▪ Adm ▪ www.creative-interactions.com

This company offers family-friendly workshops and experiences, including henna, a Medina hunt and a Moroccan Arabic class.

TOP 10 ACTIVITIES

1 Cooking
www.soukcuisine.com
Souk Cuisine organizes culinary weeks or tailor-made programmes.

2 Cycling
Bicycles can be hired across the city, including Bike Morocco at rue Khalid Ibn Eloualid in Guéliz.

3 Golf
Golf d'Amelkis: Km 12, Route de Ouarzazate; 0524 40 44 14
Play at the Palmeraie Palace (*see p117*) or the Golf d'Amelkis.

4 Hot-Air Ballooning
www.marrakechbyair.com
Marrakech By Air offers early morning balloon rides over the desert.

5 Tennis
MAP C5 ▪ Rue Oued El Makhazine, Guéliz ▪ 0524 43 19 02
The Royal Tennis Club welcomes non-members (with reservations).

6 Karting
MAP C4 ▪ 0661 23 76 87
Atlas Karting on the Route de Safi also offers quad bike rides.

7 Mountain Biking
www.marrakechbikeaction.com
In addition to full-on rough-terrain biking, MBA offers city rides.

8 Marathons
www.marathon-marrakech.com
A marathon and a half marathon take place in January.

9 Skiing
When there is snow, head for Oukaimeden in the Ourika Valley (*see p63*).

10 Quad Biking
www.dunesdesert.com
A thrilling experience for all – Dunes & Desert is one of many offering exciting quad bike adventures.

Quad biking in the desert

🔟 Nightlife

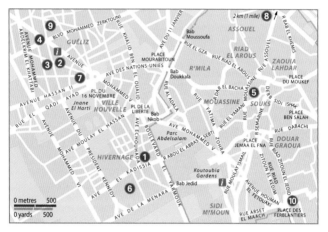

1 Comptoir Darna

A spacious lounge located above the ground-floor restaurant (see p83), with a long cocktail bar, this is the place where everyone dresses up for the evening. The atmosphere is sophisticated and elegant. There are also nightly shows featuring dance troupes, Gnawa singers or orchestras performing traditional Arab music.

Diners at Comptoir Darna

2 Kechmara

This hip café-bar (see p83) has a friendly, relaxed vibe. In addition to live music and art installations, there is beer on tap and a large food menu.

3 Sky Bab

MAP B5 ▪ Cnr blvd Mansour Eddahbi and rue Mohammed El Beqqal, Guéliz ▪ www.babhotel marrakech.ma

This rooftop bar, found at the stylish boutique Bab Hotel in central Guéliz, is spacious and cool in every sense of the word. There are DJs at the weekend and, on occasion, live music. Visitors can also order food from the tapas menu at the restaurant downstairs.

4 Sky Bar

MAP B5 ▪ 89 Angle bld Zerktouni and Mohammed V, Guéliz
Situated on the roof of La Renaissance Hotel in the heart of Guéliz, this is one of the most buzzing bars in town at the weekend. Seven storeys above place Abdel Moumen Ben Ali, it offers terrific views down Mohammed V back to the Medina. On a clear day, you can see the Atlas mountains.

5 Café Arabe

Due to the presence of several saints' shrines, the serving of alcohol in the Medina is severely restricted, limited to just a handful of venues that predominantly cater to foreign travellers. The casual Café Arabe *(see p77)* serves Moroccan and Italian food but you can drink without eating on one of its terraces or in the courtyard.

6 Théatro

MAP C6 ■ Hotel Es Saadi, ave El Kadissia, Hivernage ■ 0664 86 03 39 ■ Open 11pm–5am daily ■ MC, V accepted ■ www.theatromarrakech.com

Set in a converted music hall, this chic, popular nightclub is known for its uproarious hedonism. The former stage is now a busy dance floor, with a full schedule of resident and international DJs, and hip-hop acts. Advance booking is recommended.

7 Barométre

MAP B4 ■ Rue Moulay Ali, Guéliz ■ Open 6:30pm–1am Mon–Sat ■ www.lebarometre.net

Cocktail lovers won't be disappointed with a visit to this basement bar where mixologists create innovative drinks. Ask for a custom cocktail to be made for you or choose from the selection of classic ones on offer. Barométre also has a restaurant that serves great food.

8 Nikki Beach

Circuit de la Palmeraie ■ 0664 29 29 45 ■ Open Mar–Jan: 11:30am–8pm daily ■ MC, V accepted ■ www.palmeraieresorts.com

Lounge by the pool and swim out to the "floating bars" at this fabulously glitzy club just 15 minutes from the Medina. Although it closes at 8pm, this is a popular spot for an early-evening drink.

The pool at Nikki Beach

The lovely Grand Café de la Poste

9 Grand Café de la Poste

This beautifully converted villa was originally a French-colonial-era post office, which was built in 1925. It has a brasserie-like feel and does a busy lunch and dinner trade, but in the early evening, the terrace out front is the ideal place for a sundowner by the place du 16 Novembre *(see p83)*.

10 Kosybar

Located in the heart of the Medina, this establishment *(see p71)* features a ground floor with a piano and an elegant bar, plus a first floor with cosy nooks. Head to the roof terrace for picturesque views of the stork nests around the wall of the Badii Palace and Koutoubia Mosque.

TOP 10 Moroccan Cuisine

A colourful Moroccan salad

1 Moroccan Salads

Moroccan salads are traditionally part of a meal. Usually, one to three different small salads are served. These are made up of fresh vegetables, such as carrots, bell peppers, zucchini and tomatoes.

2 Mint Tea

The ubiquitous green tea made with fresh mint leaves is invariably served with vast quantities of sugar. The technique of pouring is almost as crucial as the drink itself; the long, curved teapot spout allows the tea to be poured theatrically, and the tradition is to have three glasses each.

Mint tea

3 Breads

There are various types of breads available that are traditionally served with every meal. *Khobz* (a small round loaf) is generally accompanied with main dishes, while *msemmen* (flatbread) is served for breakfast. The *rghaif* (bread stuffed with beef and spices) is a popular afternoon snack.

4 Briouats

Small triangles of filo pastry filled with a variety of flavours – the most common are spiced minced lamb with pine nuts and feta cheese with spinach. Some kitchens in Marrakech also prepare them with shrimp, chicken and lemon. A sweet version, filled with groundnuts and soaked in honey, is widely available.

5 Couscous

A staple cuisine across North Africa, couscous comprises tiny grains of semolina that are cooked by steaming, causing them to swell and turn light and fluffy. It is usually eaten with a spicy, harissa-flavoured broth and served with steamed vegetables and meat.

6 Pastilla

Eaten both as a starter as well as a main dish, *Pastilla* is a pillow of filo pastry filled with a sweet and savoury stuffing, generally shredded chicken or pigeon cooked with onions and a range of spices. The dish is dusted all over with cinnamon and sugar for a distinctive Moroccan flavour.

A pigeon-stuffed *pastilla*

7 Tangia

This meat-heavy dish was born in the souks of Marrakech by workmen. It is an iconic dish of slow-cooked lamb or beef with preserved lemons, garlic and saffron. The meat is then slow-cooked in the coals of the hammam furnace overnight, until it falls apart.

8 Harira

A traditional Moroccan soup made with tomatoes, lentils, chickpeas, spices and lamb, this is a substantial meal by itself. Associated with special occasions, it is served during Ramadan when it is eaten at sundown to break the fast.

A comforting bowl of harira

9 Moroccan Pastries

The popular honey cakes or *chabakia*, deep-fried and dipped in honey, are served during Ramadan. Another tasty treat is sweet *pastilla* – a filo pastry covered in nuts and *crème anglaise* (custard).

10 Tajines

Cooked slowly at a low temperature in a clay pot with a cone-shaped lid that gives the dish its name, a tajine typically combines meat with fruits. Ingredients for these stewed dishes include any foodstuff that braises well, such as fish, beef, dried fruits, olives and vegetables.

TOP 10 VARIATIONS ON A TAJINE

Beef with fennel and peas

1 Beef with fennel and peas
The chefs at La Maison Arabe's Le Restaurant *(see p77)* make good use of beef in this extremely tasty tajine.

2 Lamb, onions and almonds
This savoury lamb tajine is a classic in Marrakech.

3 Lamb and dates
Served at Le Tanjia *(see p71)* and widely used in French cuisine.

4 Lamb and pear
Soft and tender, the pear is cooked so that it all but melts to the consistency of a purée.

5 Veal and green peas
The added saffron and ginger give this tajine a very special taste.

6 Lamb, prune and roast almonds
The sliced almonds add crunch to the sticky consistency of the prunes.

7 Veal and quince
Those who like a mixture of sweet and sour should try this popular tajine.

8 Fish
Apart from at Dar Moha *(see p77),* you will find the best, freshest fish tajines in Essaouira.

9 Lamb and artichokes
Strong-flavoured seasoned lamb works beautifully with caramelised onions and fresh artichokes.

10 Kefta tajine
These are small balls of spicy minced meat that are cooked slowly in a rich tomato sauce. An egg is occasionally added to the dish.

Kefta tajine

Restaurants

Dining area at Le Foundouk

1 Le Foundouk

This stylish restaurant *(see p77)* serves fine French and Moroccan cuisine. The old courtyard building has been given a modern look, complete with leather seating and a chandelier. With a small bar area and a beautiful roof terrace, it's easy to find the perfect spot for an apéritif while waiting for a table.

2 Comptoir Darna

Located in a two-storey villa, this is a great spot *(see p83)* for a night out. The noise levels are high, with voices competing with the DJ, the food is good, with Moroccan and French choices, but it is the ambience that makes Comptoir Darna truly memorable – especially at weekends when there are belly dancers.

3 Al Fassia

This completely female-run Moroccan restaurant *(see p83)* is unusual in that it offers à la carte choices rather than a set menu. The restaurant has a charming garden but lacks the panache of its many competitors, though it compensates with its terrific local food.

4 Nomad

The clean, modern lines and restrained colour palate of this restaurant *(see p77)* are echoed in the menu, which favours fresh, contemporary flavours as traditional Moroccan dishes are given a modern makeover. It also does superb cocktails, while profits from the daily special go to a local charity.

5 Pepe Nero

Many Marrakech restaurants have beautiful riad settings but this *(see p71)* is definitely one of the most attractive, with seating around a rose-petal-strewn pool. The mixed menu of Italian and Moroccan dishes may raise eyebrows, but the food is every bit as beguiling and assured as the spectacular setting.

Cosy setting at Comptoir Darna

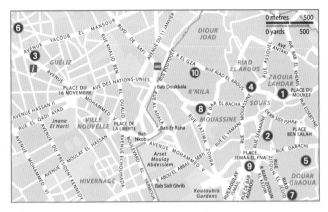

6 Amal
A charity that supports disadvantaged women, non-profit Amal (see p83) provides lunches of "home-cooked" Moroccan cuisine. The menu is limited to daily specials, however, the food is outstanding and offers terrific value. Located a little out of the way, the restaurant is five minutes' walk north of central Guéliz.

7 La Famille
In the noisy heart of the Medina, this restaurant (see p77) provides peaceful respite to the hustle and bustle, with its cool courtyard filled with banana and olive trees. The seasonal vegetarian menu focuses on inventive Mediterranean cuisine, specialising in fresh, zesty salads.

8 Dar Moha
Taste Moroccan cuisine with a modern twist by Marrakech's celebrity chef Moha Fedal. The innovative food here is unlike anything else you will eat in the city. Musicians add to the ambience and perform by the candlelit pool during summer (see p77).

9 Jemaa el Fna
Each evening a part of the main square (see pp14–15) in the Medina is transformed into a vast open-air restaurant (see p71).

People flit between the numerous makeshift kitchens that have been set up to serve the crowds, and it is possible to sample most Moroccan classics, from harira and *brochettes* to couscous and tajines.

A food stall at Jemaa el Fna

10 Le Comptoir du Pacha
Offering Moroccan and Mediterranean flavours that blend seamlessly, Le Comptoir du Pacha (see p77) is an intimate and innovative restaurant that takes you on a memorable gastronomical journey. Choose from several delicacies such as the lamb shoulder, that's been cooked to perfection, or a tajine with duck confit. There are vegetarian options available too.

Day Trips

 Country Markets
Several small villages in the vicinity of Marrakech host weekly markets, with villagers from surrounding regions flocking to buy and sell produce, cheap clothing and assorted bric-a-brac. Cattle auctions are also common, as are makeshift salons of travelling barbers and dentists. Donkeys and mules are the dominant means of transport. Ask your hotel for details on where and when to find them.

2 Setti Fatma
MAP C2
This small hidden village is a 90-minute drive to the south of the city. Here, at the head of the Ourika Valley in the foothills of the Atlas Mountains, visitors will find the starting point for a 15-minute stroll up to a fine waterfall and pool. Beyond this is a strenuous hike up a steep, rocky valley to six more waterfalls.

3 Tin Mal
About a two-hour drive south of Marrakech on R203, the ancient mosque *(see p94)* of Tin Mal makes for a stunning day out if a full trip over the Tizi-n-Test pass is not possible. Travel on a Saturday and you can stop at Asni's weekly market en route.

The stunning Cascades d'Ouzoud

4 Cascades d'Ouzoud
MAP D1 ■ Riad Cascades d'Ouzoud ■ 0523 42 91 73 ■ www. ouzoud.com
Two hours northeast on the Route de Fès, these are the most beautiful waterfalls in Morocco. Take a trek through wooded groves *(ouzoud* is Amazigh for olives) to reach the gorges of Oued El Abid. There is a lovely riad at the top of the cascades if you fancy spending the night.

5 Essaouira
This medieval walled port-city on the Atlantic coast is only a few hours' drive from Marrakech. It has beaches, ramparts, souks, a fishing harbour and a fascinating hippy-era history *(see pp86–91)*.

6 Tameslouht
MAP C1
A 30-minute drive out of Marrakech on the Route d'Amizmiz, Tameslouht is a roadside village famed

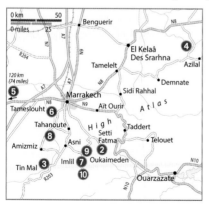

for its busy potters' cooperative. There are also weavers' workshops, an ancient mule-driven olive oil press and a crumbling kasbah. Start the trip with a visit to the Association Tameslouht – a useful information office on the main square, place Sour Souika, next to the main mosque. If the office is shut, one of the locals will be able to tell you where to find the potters.

Visitors skiing at Oukaimeden

7 Imlil
MAP C2

An hour-and-a-half drive from Marrakech, the mountain village of Imlil sits at the head of the Aït Mizane Valley in the High Atlas. Its altitude makes it a popular base for hiking. Most people come here to tackle nearby Jbel Toubkal *(see p93)*, but there are many other hikes of differing lengths and degrees of difficulty.

8 Barrage Lalla Takerkoust
MAP C2 ▪ Le Flouka, BP 45 Barrage Lalla Takerkoust ▪ 0664 49 26 60 ▪ www.leflouka-marrakech.com

Found to the south of Marrakech on the Route d'Amizmiz, this impressive artificial lake is backed by the beautiful Atlas Mountains. The clear water makes it a great place for a relaxing lakeside picnic. It is also popular with quad bikers. Try the local cuisine at one of the many waterside restaurants, including Le Flouka, which also offers accommodation.

9 Oukaimeden
MAP C2

Snowfall on the Atlas between February and April means business for the ski resort at Oukaimeden, high above the Ourika Valley. There is a chairlift and ski equipment can be hired on site. In spring and summer, visitors can see the Bronze Age petroglyphs.

10 Kasbah du Toubkal
A former tribal stronghold deep in the Atlas Mountains, this traditional kasbah is set at the foot of Jbel Toubkal *(see p93)*. The last part of the journey is done by mule. Visitors are brought up for an Amazigh lunch and hike, and are dropped back into town before dark. It is possible to stay overnight at the kasbah *(see p97)*.

Kasbah du Toubkal

Marrakech
Area by Area

The UNESCO World Heritage Site
Kasbah Aït Benhaddou

TOP 10 Jemaa el Fna and the Kasbah

Dar Si Said Museum detail

The spiritual and historical heart of Marrakech, the Jemaa el Fna (pronounced as a rushed "j'maf na"), was laid out as a parade ground by the founders of the city. Marrakech's next rulers constructed a walled royal domain to the south – known as the Kasbah – and the open ground passed into the public domain. Sultans and royal palaces have come and gone, but the Jemaa el Fna remains eternally vital and has long been the center for commerce in Marrakech. It is home to lively sights, traditional Gnawa musicians and colourful juice carts. By night, it transforms into a food market.

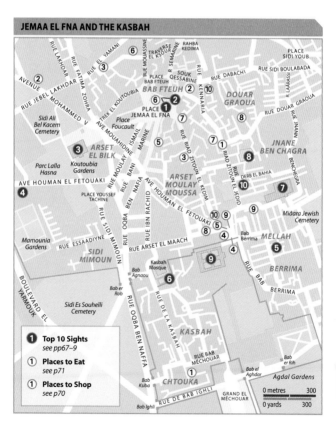

JEMAA EL FNA AND THE KASBAH

Top 10 Sights
see pp67–9

Places to Eat
see p71

Places to Shop
see p70

1 Jemaa el Fna

One of the most spectacular squares in North Africa, Jemaa el Fna throngs with entertainers and locals as well as enthralled visitors from all over the world. Running south off Jemma el Fna, Rue de Bab Agnaou is the Medina's pedestrianized "modern" main street, where you can find ATMs, internet cafés and pharmacies. Its narrow side alleys are home to good-value hotels (see pp12–13).

2 Night Market

Early evening brings a change to Jemaa el Fna as the nightly food market takes over the square and fills the air with the aroma of grilling meat. Nearby is the Rue Riad Zitoun el Jedid, which connects several major sights with Jemaa el Fna, including the Dar Si Said Museum. Rue Riad Zitoun el Kedim links Jemaa el Fna with the palace quarter (see pp14–15).

3 Koutoubia Mosque

The Koutoubia Mosque is easily identified by its magnificent minaret (tower). This beautiful structure reaches a towering height of 77 m (252 ft), its rose-pink colour makes for an eye-catching contrast, silhouetted against the cobalt blue of the sky by day and the fiery orange of twilight in the early evening (see pp20–21). Although, only Muslims are permitted inside the mosque, one of the doors on the east wall is often open, so visitors can peer through for a view.

Koutoubia Mosque

4 La Mamounia Hotel

This former palace has been one of Marrakech's landmark hotels (see pp34–5) since it opened in 1923. While it has a reputation of hosting celebrities and famous visitors such as Winston Churchill, you don't have to be a guest to enjoy its poolside bar and restaurant – just dress the part.

Al Mamoun Suite, La Mamounia Hotel

5 The Mellah
MAP L5

The old Jewish quarter lies immediately east of the Kasbah. Visitors can enter via the Souk El Bab Salaam, a busy, covered market street across from a rose-planted square. The street leads to place Souweka and to the north you'll find one of the city's last working synagogues. Most of Marrakech's Jewish population left for Israel after World War II, in the 1950s and 1960s, but the number of graves in the nearby Miâara Jewish cemetery is testament to how many once lived here.

6 Saadian Tombs

MAP J6 ■ Rue de la Kasbah, Medina ■ Open 9am–2:30pm daily ■ Adm

The historic Saadian tombs are located down a narrow alley that runs beside the Kasbah Mosque, which itself is just inside the beautiful and equally historic Bab Agnaou *(see p25)*. The small garden site is the resting place for some 66 royals of the Saadian dynasty, whose reign marked a golden era in the history of the city. This site can get easily crowded. Visit early morning or late afternoon for the best chance of avoiding the rush.

Saadian Tombs and garden

7 Bahia Palace

Built in the 1890s by a powerful grand vizier (high official), the Bahia *(see pp26–7)* is an impressive minor palace complex approached by a long garden driveway. Inside, arrows direct visitors through a succession of courtyards and private rooms that were used by the vizier and his four wives. All of the rooms are lavishly decorated with *zellij* tiling *(see p41)*, sculpted stucco and carved cedarwood. The ruling sultan, Abdel Aziz, was so jealous of the riches of the Bahia that on the vizier's death he had parts of the palace stripped.

8 Dar Si Said Museum

MAP K4 ■ Rue Riad Zitoun El Jedid ■ 0524 38 95 64 ■ Open 9am–5pm Wed–Mon ■ Adm

Built by the brother of Ba Ahmed, builder of the Bahia Palace, this is an altogether more modest dwelling. However, what it sacrifices in scale, it more than makes up for in its impressive detailing – the house has some beautiful painted ceilings. It also serves as a museum for decorative arts; the exhibits on display include fine examples of carved wooden panels and painted Amazigh doors. The museum also houses some interestingly designed jewellery, carpets and metalwork.

9 Badii Palace

It is difficult to reconcile these ruins *(see pp30–31)* with a palace once reputed to be among the world's finest. An expanse of dusty ground within half-eroded walls, it retains some of its original elements, including sunken gardens and dazzling Moorish craftsmanship.

Bahia Palace decoration

Exhibits at Musée Tiskiwin

⑩ Musée Tiskiwin
MAP K4 ▪ 8 derb El Bahia, off rue Riad Zitoun El Jedid ▪ 0524 38 91 92 ▪ Open 9am–12:30pm & 2:30–6pm daily ▪ Adm

Located en route to the Dar Si Said Museum, this is a private house belonging to the Dutch anthropologist Bert Flint. An avid documenter of tribal arts and crafts, Flint amassed a fascinating and vast collection. Presented in his home for public viewing, the exhibition has been organized geographically as a journey that traces the old desert trade routes all the way from Marrakech to Timbuktu. Exhibit labels are in French, but there is an English guidebook.

THE KING AND HIS PALACES
Throughout Moroccan history, the royal court has shifted base between Marrakech, Fès, Meknès and Rabat. The Almohads constructed Marrakech's first royal palace in the 12th century to the south of Jemaa el Fna and it has been there ever since. The present King Mohammed VI had a smaller palace built for his personal use, outside the Bab Agnaou.

TO THE PALACES

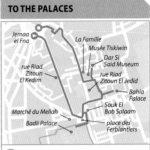

▶ MORNING

Start on **Jemaa el Fna** *(see pp12–15)*. On the southern side is an arch that leads to rue Riad Zitoun El Kedim. This area is mainly inhabited by locals and there is a distinct absence of souvenir and trinket vendors. At the southern end of the street, several places sell items that are fashioned out of old car tyres – from the purely practical (buckets) to the quirky (stylish mirror frames). Across the main road is the **Marché du Mellah** *(see p70)*, a fruit, vegetable and meat market that's worth a quick look. Just southeast is the **Place des Ferblantiers** *(see p70)*, a paved plaza surrounded by metalworkers with a gate that leads through to the haunting **Badii Palace**. After visiting the ruins, grab a cheap snack from one of the stalls on the northwest corner of place des Ferblantiers.

AFTERNOON

Wander through the **Souk El Bab Salaam** *(see p70)* before heading back north up the **rue Riad Zitoun El Jedid**. At the end of the street, on the right, is the gateway to the **Bahia Palace**, but anyone pushed for time should instead turn right and take the first left to the excellent **Dar Si Said Museum**. Just south is the equally interesting **Musée Tiskiwin**. Return to rue Riad Zitoun El Jedid and continue north where you will eventually reach **La Famille** *(see p77)*, a tranquil spot where you can pause to have refreshing mint tea. Bear to the left to re-emerge onto the lively Jemaa el Fna.

See map on p66 ←

Places to Shop

A woman walks past Moroccan carpets on rue Riad Zitoun El Jedid

1 Rue Riad Zitoun El Jedid
MAP K4

This street is lined with small, interesting boutiques. It is a pleasant alternative to the souks.

2 Ensemble Artisanal Marrakech
MAP H3 ■ Ave Mohammed V

This government-run shop is a short walk from Jemaa el Fna. You'll find traditional Moroccan handicrafts at fixed prices here, so no haggling.

3 RAQAS
MAP J3 ■ 1 rue el Ksour

Stylish Moroccan clothing is on offer at the store of this fair-trade fashion brand. Custom tailoring is available and there are accessories for sale too.

4 Place des Ferblantiers
MAP K5

As an alternative to the souks, this is the place to go to for unique brass and iron lanterns that come in all shapes and sizes.

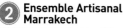

Brass lantern

5 Aya's
MAP K5 ■ 11 bis, derb Jdid, Bab Mellah ■ www.ayasmarrakech.com

It may be hard to find (a door away from Le Tanjia), but it is worth seeking out for clothing, jewellery and accessories.

6 AlNour
MAP J3 ■ Derb Moulay El Ghali 19 ■ 0524 39 03 23

This social enterprise boutique features exquisite accessories and hand-embroidered clothing made with natural fibers, crafted by local women.

7 Le Cadeau Berbère
MAP J3 ■ 51 Jemaa el Fna ■ 0524 44 29 07

Established in 1930, this family-run textile specialist has an international clientele that includes interior designers, hoteliers and collectors.

8 Marché du Mellah
MAP K5 ■ Ave Houman El Fetouaki ■ Closed Fri

This indoor market sells flowers, household goods and local produce.

9 Atelier El Bahia
MAP K5 ■ Rue Bahia Bab Mellah ■ 0524 38 52 86

Even if you're not in the market for a new rug, you can still browse handmade shawls, throws and soft furnishings.

10 Souk El Bab Salaam
MAP K5

Follow the aromas wafting from the edge of the old Jewish quarter to this small herb and spice market in Place des Ferblantiers.

Places to Eat

PRICE CATEGORIES

For a full meal for one with half a bottle of wine (or equivalent meal), plus taxes and extra charges.

Dh under 200 Dh   Dh Dh 200–400 Dh
Dh Dh Dh over 400 Dh

1 Café Clock
MAP K7 ▪ 224 derb Chtouka, Kasbah ▪ 0524 37 83 67 ▪ Open 9am–10pm daily ▪ Dh

Serving camel burgers, almond milkshakes, homemade ice cream and all-day Amazigh breakfasts.

2 Le Marrakchi
MAP K3 ▪ 52 rue des Banques ▪ 0524 44 33 77 ▪ Open noon–midnight daily ▪ MC, V accepted ▪ Dh Dh Dh

This restaurant has a lively roof terrace, with music and belly dancing.

3 Marrakech Henna Art Café
MAP K4 ▪ 36 derb Sqaya ▪ 0524 38 14 10 ▪ Open noon–8pm Mon, Tue & Thu–Sun ▪ Credit cards accepted ▪ Dh

Moroccan dishes, including vegetarian and vegan options, are served here. Organic henna application available.

4 Kosybar
MAP K5 ▪ 47 place des Ferblantiers ▪ 0524 38 03 24 ▪ Open 11:30am–1am daily ▪ MC, V accepted ▪ Dh Dh Dh

Eat Japanese-Mediterranean fusion on the lovely, cool terrace or in the elegant interior of this restaurant.

5 Pâtisserie des Princes
MAP J4 ▪ Passage Prince Moulay Rachid ▪ 0524 44 30 33 ▪ Open 7am–11pm daily ▪ Dh

A local version of a French pastry parlour, this place also offers ice creams, juices, tea and coffee.

6 Jemaa el Fna
For the ultimate dining experience, try one of the stalls in the square (see pp14–15).

7 Naranj
MAP K4 ▪ 84 rue Riad Zitoun el Jdid ▪ 0524 38 68 05 ▪ Open noon–10pm Mon–Sat ▪ Credit cards accepted ▪ Dh Dh

Take a break from tajines at this beautiful Lebanese spot serving flavourful dishes.

8 Pepe Nero
MAP K4 ▪ 17 derb Cherkaoui, Douar Graoua ▪ 0524 38 90 67 ▪ Open 7:30–11:30pm Tue–Sun; lunch by pre-booking only ▪ Dh Dh Dh

Excellent high-end Italian-Moroccan, worth splashing out on (see p60).

High-end dining at Pepe Nero

9 Le Tanjia
MAP K5 ▪ 14 derb Jedid, Hay Essalam, Mellah ▪ 0524 38 38 36 ▪ Open noon–midnight daily ▪ Credit cards accepted ▪ Dh Dh Dh

A three-floored temple of fine dining and entertainment with an excellent Moroccan menu and belly dancers.

10 Roti d'Or
MAP K3 ▪ 17 rue Kennaria, Medina ▪ 0627 13 11 37 ▪ Open noon–4pm & 6–8:30pm Sat–Thu ▪ Dh

A small but hip pavement café, Roti d'Or offers a wide range of burgers, tacos and wraps that are prepared with a Moroccan twist.

See map on p66 ←

TOP 10 The Souks

North of Jemaa el Fna is a vast area of tightly squeezed commerce with dozens of narrow alleyways. These passageways are lined with shops the size of cupboards selling cloth, leather, metalwork, brass lanterns, carpets and jewellery. Each area is dedicated to a single item, so a street may be packed with sellers of nothing but canary-yellow leather slippers, while another is filled with vendors of glazed pottery. A trip to the souks is an endurance test of just how long you can keep your money in your pocket. Come prepared to bargain, it's part of how the souk economy works.

Mouassine Fountain

1 Mouassine Fountain
MAP J2

There are two main routes into the souks: rue Mouassine and rue Semmarine. The former runs past the Mouassine Mosque, after which the neighbourhood is named. A right turn at the mosque leads to a small plaza that holds a fountain with four bays – three for animals and one for humans. An arched gateway next to the fountain leads to the Souk des Teinturiers.

2 Dar Cherifa
MAP J2 ■ 8 derb Charfa Lakbir, Mouassine ■ 0524 42 65 50 ■ Open 10am–midnight Thu–Tue, 10am–7pm Wed ■ www.dar-cherifa.com

This beautifully renovated townhouse can be located by following the signs on the alley opposite the Mouassine Mosque. Featuring exquisite wood-work and carved plasterwork, some of the interiors date back to the 16th century. The house operates as a cultural centre, restaurant and *salon de thé* (tearoom).

3 Fondouks
MAP J2 ■ 192 rue Mouassine

To the north of the Mouassine Mosque, past Café Arabe *(see p77)*, is an excellent example of a *fondouk* – an old merchants' hostel. The rooms on the ground floor are used as workshops and the ones upstairs are mainly used for storage.

THE SOUKS

[map of the souks showing streets including DERB SIDI MESSOUD SGHIR, RUE EL GZA, ARSET IHIRI, DERB SIDI BOU AMEUR, BHOUWZ, ARSET BEN CHEBLI, DERB SIDI BOU AM, JDID, DERB SIDI LAKHEN OU ALI, SIDI BOU AMEUR, RUE R'MILA, BAB, RUE RIAD LAARROUS, DERB DEKKAK, DOU KKALA, ARSET AGUZAL, RUE AL ADALA, JBEL LAHKDAR, RUE FATIMA ZOHRA, RUE DAR EL BACHA, Dar el Bacha, RUE JEBEL LAKHDAR, RUE FATIMA ZOHRA, RUE EL YAN, AVENUE MOHAMMED V, Arset Moulay Abdesslem, RUE JEBEL LAKHDAR, EL KSOUR)

This particular *fondouk* had a brush with stardom when it featured in the 1998 film *Hideous Kinky*, as the hotel where actress Kate Winslet and her daughters are shown to be staying.

4 Souk des Teinturiers

One of the most alluring places in Marrakech, the Dyers' Souk *(see p16)* is a tangle of narrow alleyways east of the Mouassine Mosque. It becomes a riot of colours during the day, when hanks of just-dyed wools are hung out to dry above certain alleys. The dyers themselves are very easy to identify; they are the men with bright red, purple and blue colours up to their elbows.

Dyed wool hanging in Souk des Teinturiers

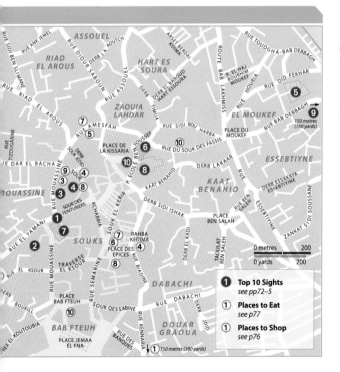

- **1** Top 10 Sights
  see pp72–5

- **1** Places to Eat
  see p77

- **1** Places to Shop
  see p76

The wonderfully colourful, but overwhelmingly pungent, tanneries

5 The Tanneries
MAP L1

A strong stomach is required to visit this particular quarter of the Medina. This is where animal hides are turned into leather. The work is done by hand as the hides are soaked in open vats. They look like a paintbox of watercolours from a distance, but up close smell so foul that guides give visitors sprigs of mint to hold under their noses. The tanneries are scheduled to move location as a result of the pollution they cause. If you venture this far, pay a visit to the nearby Bab Debbagh *(see p25)*.

6 Medersa Ben Youssef
Located north of the Musée de Marrakech, this is a beautiful building *(see pp28–9)*. A 16th-century theological college, it has tiny, window-less cells designed to house several hundred students. The central court-yard, which combines polychromic tiling, decorative plasterwork and wood panelling to sublime effect, is its most stunning feature.

7 Musée Douiria de Mouassine
MAP J2 ▪ 4–5 derb el Hammam, Mouassine ▪ 0524 37 77 92 ▪ Open 9:30am–7pm daily ▪ Adm ▪ www.museedemouassine.com

A remarkable discovery was unearthed at this otherwise modest first-floor apartment.

Hidden beneath the plaster were extraordinary painted ceilings and panels. It emerged that this had been the residence of a Saadian noble and below the later accretions, its 16th-century architecture and decor remained intact. Visitors can view the ongoing restoration work, visit temporary exhibitions and take tea at the rooftop café.

8 Musée de Marrakech
MAP K2 ▪ Place Ben Youssef ▪ 0524 44 18 93 ▪ Open 9am–6:30pm daily (except religious holidays) ▪ Adm ▪ www.musee.ma

This splendid 19th-century palace houses the Fondation Omar Benjelloun, which features ethnological and archaeological material as well as a wide-ranging collection of ancient and con-temporary artwork. The former

Courtyard, Musée de Marrakech

hammam makes an unusual exhibition space. Books, tea, coffee and pastries are also sold here.

⑨ City Walls and Gates

The city walls and gates *(see pp24–5)*, built around the 1120s, surround the Medina. While Bab Agnaou city gate, which is located to the west of the Saadian Tombs is considered to be the most beautiful, Bab Debbagh gate gives you access to the tanneries. The internal staircase at Bab Debbagh leads to a roof from which you can enjoy stunning, panoramic views of the city.

The ancient Koubba El Badiyin

⑩ Koubba El Badiyin

MAP K2 ▪ Place Ben Youssef
▪ 0524 44 18 93 ▪ Open 8:30am–6pm Mon–Fri ▪ Adm

This fully intact building from the 11th century is the only remaining example of Almoravid architecture in the city. Built by the Almoravid dynasty, it is assumed to be the ablutions area for the Medersa Ben Youssef. Its intricate arches are reminiscent of the mosques of Andalucia, from the time of the Caliphate.

PRETTY IN PINK

Every building in the Medina is painted pink. Why? It's the law, introduced during the era of French rule. The colour is actually ochre, the colour of the earth from which bricks were made in the past. Modern buildings still uphold this pink paint tradition, making the city a photographer's dream, particularly in the morning and evening light.

HIDDEN MARRAKECH

▶ MORNING

Wrong turns and too many distractions make it impossible to plan a walk through the souks, which you should explore independently. On another day, head up rue Mouassine and take a left opposite the Mouassine Mosque before taking the first right to **Dar Cherifa** *(see p72)*. Return to rue Mouassine and turn left at the T-junction. Take the first right through a low archway; follow the alley left and then right to No. 22 and ring the bell for the eccentric **Ministero del Gusto** *(by appointment only; 0524 42 64 55)*, a gallery and concept store. Back on the main street, take a left towards the **Mouassine Fountain** *(see p72)* or detour for a look at the **Musée Douiria de Mousassine**. Head north up rue Mouassine and stop at the **Café Arabe** *(see p77)* for lunch.

AFTERNOON

After the café is the **fondouk** *(see p72)* made famous in *Hideous Kink*y starring Kate Winslet. Bear left onto rue Dar El Bacha, named for the Dar El Bacha palace, which has been converted into the Dar El Bacha Musée des Confluences. It features temporary exhibitions devoted to Islamic art, science and knowledge. Continue past the Bab Doukkala Mosque, through a street market to the **Bab Doukkala gate** *(see p25)* and exit the Medina; you could walk on to Guéliz or catch a taxi back to Jemaa el Fna.

See map on pp72–3

Places to Shop

Mustapha Blaoui
MAP H2 ▪ 142 rue Bab Doukkala ▪ 0524 38 52 40
Monsieur Blaoui's warehouse of Moroccan goods has everything from candleholders to wardrobes.

Moroccan goods, Mustapha Blaoui

2 Ensemble Artisanal
MAP H3 ▪ Ave Mohammed V ▪ 0524 44 35 03
A government store of Moroccan handicrafts. Though not as much fun as the souks, it is less stressful.

3 Kulchi
MAP J3 ▪ 15 derb Nkhel ▪ 0639 22 12 59 ▪ www.kulchi.com
A fashion-mag-friendly, Australian-owned business selling gorgeous carpets, hand-woven blankets, ceramics and other objects. By appointment.

4 Michi
MAP J2 ▪ 38 Souk el Kimakhin
Owned by a Japanese-Moroccan couple, this small shop has Moroccan homeware and artisanal goods with a Japanese style. The Moroccan slippers are particularly well made.

Sack slippers, Souk Cherifia

Max & Jan
MAP K2 ▪ 14 rue Amsefah, Sidi Abdelaziz ▪ 0661 14 62 26 ▪ www.maxandjan.com
From their flagship boutique in the Medina, Swiss-Belgian duo Max and Jan bring an international edge to Moroccan design.

Chabi Chic
MAP H2 ▪ 91 rue Lalla Fatima Zahra ▪ 0524 42 85 80
Located within Nomad restaurant, this attractive boutique sells traditional and contemporary handmade pottery as well as beauty products.

Bazar du Sud
MAP K2 ▪ 14 Souk des Tapis ▪ 0662 05 89 11 ▪ www.bazardusud.com
Of the countless carpet shops in the souk, this has possibly the largest selection, backed up by an extremely professional sales service.

L'Art du Bain
MAP K3 ▪ 13 Souk el Badine ▪ 068 44 59 42
This store deals in handmade soaps, from the traditional Moroccan *savon noir* to natural soaps infused with rose or musk.

Souk Cherifia
MAP J2 ▪ 184 rue Mouassine, Medina
One of the best shopping stops for designer clothes, accessories and homeware, composed of more than 20 independent boutiques.

10 Beldi
MAP J3 ▪ 9–11 rue Laksour ▪ 0524 44 10 76
This tiny boutique at the entrance to the souks showcases the work of brothers Toufik and Abdelhafid. They adapt Moroccan clothing for contemporary Western tastes to stunning effect.

Places to Eat

PRICE CATEGORIES
For a full meal for one with half a bottle of wine (or equivalent meal), plus taxes and extra charges.
....
 under 200 Dh   200–400 Dh
 over 400 Dh

1 La Famille
MAP K4 ▪ 42 rue Riad Zitoun el Jdid ▪ 0524 38 52 95 ▪ Open noon–3:30pm Tue–Sun ▪ Credit cards accepted ▪

Enjoy vegetarian Mediterranean cuisine in the shade of this tranquil garden restaurant that comes as a surprise in the bustle of the Medina.

2 La Maison Arabe
Moroccan cuisine in the main restaurant (see p112). French, Moroccan and Asian in Les Trois Saveurs.

3 Café Arabe
MAP J2 ▪ 184 rue Mouassine ▪ 0524 42 97 28 ▪ Open 10am–midnight daily ▪

Italian and Moroccan food is served on the pillow-strewn roof terrace.

4 L'mida
MAP K2 ▪ 78 bis derb Nkhel Rahba Kdima ▪ 0524 44 36 62 ▪ Open noon–11pm daily ▪ Credit cards accepted ▪

Enjoy modern twists on Moroccan dishes while admiring city views from the roof terrace.

5 Dar Moha
MAP H2 ▪ 81 rue Dar El Bacha ▪ 0524 38 64 00/38 62 64 ▪ Open noon–4pm, 7:30–10pm daily ▪ AmEx, MC, V accepted ▪

Sit by the pool and enjoy the exceptional food at this spot (see p61).

6 Café des Epices
MAP K3 ▪ 75 Rahba Lakdima ▪ 0524 39 17 70 ▪ Open 9am–11pm daily ▪ No credit cards ▪

Calm and charming, this café offers a welcome break from the souk.

7 Atay Café
MAP K2 ▪ 62 rue Amesfah, Sidi Abdelaziz ▪ 0661 34 42 46 ▪ Open 10am–10pm daily ▪

A beautiful, friendly little café with three terraces. As well as Moroccan staples, it serves dishes like ravioli, salads and juices.

8 Nomad
MAP K3 ▪ 1 derb Arjaan, off Rahba Kedima ▪ 0524 38 16 09 ▪ Open noon–11pm daily ▪ Credit cards accepted ▪

Excellent contemporary restaurant (see p60) owned by the same people behind Café des Épices and Terrasse des Épices above the Souk Cherifia.

9 Le Compotoir du Pacha
MAP H2 ▪ 218 rue Arset Aouzal ▪ 0524 38 39 16 ▪ Open noon–11:30pm daily ▪ Credit cards accepted ▪

Savour Moroccan and Mediterranean cuisine at this restuarant (see p61). Along with scrumptious meat dishes, a vegetarian menu is also offered.

Diners on roof terrace of Le Foundouk

10 Le Foundouk
MAP K2 ▪ 55 rue du Souk des Fassis ▪ 0524 37 81 90 ▪ Open 7pm–midnight Thu–Tue ▪ MC, V accepted ▪

Wonderfully stylish restaurant (see p60) with a French-Moroccan menu. There's also a romantic roof terrace.

See map on pp72–3

🔟 **The New City**

It was only with the arrival of the French in the early 20th century that Marrakech broke out of the walls of the Medina. The new colonial rulers built their own *ville nouvelle* of broad avenues, villas and parks. Over time, Moroccans aspiring for a better lifestyle moved out into this new town, lured by serviceable plumbing, electricity and cars. Now known as Guéliz – from *église*, French for church (the area has the city's first) – the New City has plenty for tourists looking to explore Marrakech's modern facet. The streets are lined with fine restaurants and shops, while come evening, there is a lively nightlife.

Jnane El Harti

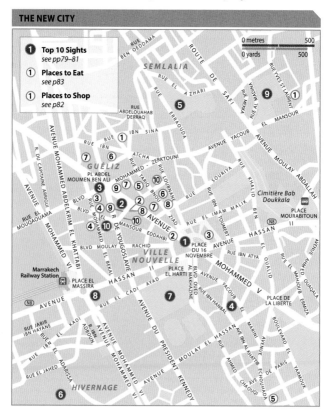

THE NEW CITY

- 1 **Top 10 Sights** see pp79–81
- 1 **Places to Eat** see p83
- 1 **Places to Shop** see p82

Avenue Mohammed V, a grand, palm-shaded thoroughfare through the city

① Avenue Mohammed V
MAP C5

This wide avenue, named after Mohamed V, is the spine of Marrakech. It connects the old and new cities, running from the Koutoubia to Jbel Guéliz (Mount Guéliz), a rocky outcrop northwest of the town. Along the way are three major roundabouts: place de la Liberté with its modern fountain; place du 16 Novembre where the main post office is located; and the heart of the New City, place Abdel Moumen Ben Ali.

② Mauresque Architecture
The French brought with them European architectural styles, which mixed with local Moorish influences to create a new style, soon dubbed "Mauresque". Avenue Mohammed V is dotted with Mauresque structures, especially where it intersects with rue de la Liberté; here several buildings have clean Modernist lines but also have pavement arcades to shade pedestrians from the sun.

③ Hotel La Renaissance
MAP C5 ■ 89 Angle blvd Zerktouni and Mohammed V, Guéliz ■ 0524 33 77 77 ■ www.renaissance-hotel-marrakech.com

Built in 1952, La Renaissance was the first hotel in the modern district of Guéliz, and has since become an iconic building in Marrakech. The rooftop terrace offers a breathtaking panorama of the whole of the Guéliz area, and is the perfect spot to sample cocktails and take in the splendour of the Koutoubia *(see p56)*.

④ Église des Saints-Martyrs de Marrakech
MAP C5 ■ Rue El Imam Ali, Guéliz ■ 0524 43 05 85 ■ Services: 6:30pm Mon–Sat, 10am Sun

Built in 1926, this Catholic church stands as a tribute to six 13th-century Franciscan friars beheaded by the sultan as a punishment for preaching Christianity. Its spartan interior is enlivened by colourful panels of stained glass. The church's bell tower is now overshadowed by the minaret of an adjacent mosque. Protestant services are held in the library on Sunday at 10:30am.

Serene interior of Église des Saints-Martyrs de Marrakech

The European cemetery

5 European Cemetery
MAP C4 ■ Rue Erraouda
■ Open Apr–Sep: 7am–7pm daily;
Oct–Mar: 8am–6pm daily

North of boulevard Mohammed Zerktouni is a walled graveyard dating back to the 1920s. It is the burial ground of many of the original inhabitants of Guéliz. A dozen English Protestant missionaries also rest here. Most notable is the tomb of Kate Hosali, who founded SPANA, a charity for working animals of the world, in 1923 after being appalled by the maltreatment of Morocco's beasts of burden.

6 Hivernage
MAP C6

South of Guéliz and immediately west of the Medina walls, Hivernage is a small neighbourhood of quiet streets that are shaded by trees. Its mix of villas and some five-star hotels ensures a tranquil atmosphere with light pedestrian traffic.

There are one or two fairly good restaurants in the area, in addition to one of the city's favourite night-spots, Comptoir Darna *(see p56)*.

7 Jnane El Harti
MAP C5

A small and pretty park just off place du 16 Novembre, Jnane El Harti was originally laid out by the French as a formal garden and zoo. In a 1939 essay titled "Marrakech", George Orwell *(see p44)* writes of feeding gazelles here. Numerous notices provide information about the various species of plants growing in the many flowerbeds. The plaza fronting the park gates is popular and often used for events.

MOVIE TIME

The city has been a popular Hollywood film location since the 1950s and it continues to star in blockbusters, including *Sex and the City 2* (2010) and *Men in Black: International* (2019). Movie buffs and the rich and famous descend on Hivernage in December for the Marrakech International Film Festival. Special events are held across the city.

---

8 Théâtre Royal
MAP B5 ■ Ave Hassan II ■ 0524 43 15 16 ■ Opening times vary

This striking piece of architecture by leading local light, Charles Boccara, is crowned by a grand dome. The interior has a beautiful,

Théâtre Royal

tiled courtyard linking a 1,200-seat open-air theatre and an 800-seat opera house. The work of local artists and sculptors is occasionally displayed here.

Majorelle Gardens fountain

⑨ Majorelle Gardens

A 10-minute walk east of place Abdel Moumen Ben Ali, these gardens *(see pp32–3)* are the absolute must-see sight in the New City. Created in the 1920s and 1930s by the French painter Jacques Majorelle, they were owned by French couturier Yves Saint-Laurent until his death in 2008. Open to the public, the gardens include a museum of Amazigh culture, a gift shop, gallery, café and a garden memorial to YSL. Next door is the Musée Yves Saint Laurent.

⑩ Spanish Quarter
MAP B5

Running west off rue de Yougoslavie is a narrow street lined with single-storey houses of a unique design, much like terraced cottages. This shady lane, planted with mulberry trees, constitutes the city's old Spanish quarter, a testament to Marrakech's once considerable Hispanic population. The small houses, formerly brightly coloured, are now a uniform Marrakech pink.

OLD CITY TO NEW CITY

Les Négociants
rue de la Liberté
Marché Central
place de la Liberté
Grand Café de la Poste
Bab Nkob
Jnane El Harti
Église des Sts-Martyrs de Marrakech
Arsat Moulay Abdeslem
avenue Mohammed V
Koutoubia Mosque

▶ MORNING

Start next to the **Koutoubia Mosque** *(see pp20–21)* and head up **avenue Mohammed V** *(see p79)*. After a few minutes you will come to **Arsat Moulay Abdeslem** *(see p51)* on the left, known as "Cyber Park" after its popular internet centre. Exit the Medina through the Bab Nkob, plunging into the large traffic island, place de la Liberté. Take the second left after the traffic junction, followed by the first right, and you'll find yourself in the historic **Église des Saints-Martyrs de Marrakech** *(see p79)*. Continue north up avenue Yacoub Marini to reach **Jnane El Harti** park. Cross the place du 16 Novembre to lunch at the **Grand Café de la Poste** *(see p83)*.

AFTERNOON

The road next to McDonald's leads to the **Marché Central** *(see p82)* which is well worth the 15-minute detour. Return to Mohammed V for some of the best shopping in town, particularly around rue de la Liberté, just past the Carré Eden shopping centre. The next major traffic intersection, place Abdel Moumen Ben Ali, is overlooked by the Parisian-style **Café Les Négociants** *(see p83)* which is a good place to rest your feet and enjoy a coffee or an orange juice. You are now at the heart of Guéliz; in addition to shopping, there are several interesting galleries nearby *(see pp42–3)*, as well as excellent eating and drinking options *(see p83)*.

See map on p78 »

Places to Shop

1 33 Rue Majorelle
MAP C4 ▪ 33 rue Yves Saint-Laurent, Guéliz ▪ 0524 31 41 95
▪ www.33ruemajorelle.com
Regularly changing stock from a host of Moroccan designers including clothes, accessories, jewellery and handicrafts.

Accessories at 33 Rue Majorelle

2 Place Vendôme
MAP B5 ▪ 141 ave Mohammed V ▪ 0524 43 52 63 ▪ Open 9am–1pm & 3–7pm daily ▪ MC, V accepted
The leather items here are of much greater quality than those sold in the souks and are designed with more of an international style and flavour.

3 Marché Central
MAP C4 ▪ Rue Ibn Toumert
A variety of foodstuffs are available at this market (see p53), as well as traditional handicrafts.

4 Maison ARTC
MAP B5 ▪ 96 rue Mohammed el Beqal ▪ 0524 38 14 27 ▪ Open 11am–8pm Mon–Sat (by appointment only) ▪ Credit cards accepted
Run by the visionary Moroccan-Israeli designer Artsi Ifrach, Maison ARTC

stocks an eclectic range of clothing items, noted for their vibrant patterns and outlandish charm.

5 Moor
MAP B5 ▪ 7 rue des Vieux Marrakchis, Guéliz ▪ 0524 45 82 74
▪ Closed Sun ▪ Credit cards accepted
▪ www.akbardelightscollections.com
Sublime clothing and houseware, though it can be a little pricey.

6 Café du Livre
MAP B5 ▪ 44 rue Tarik Bnou Ziad ▪ 0524 44 69 21 ▪ Closed Sun
▪ Credit cards accepted
A haven for book lovers offering a range of titles from across the globe. It also has a café with Wi-Fi access.

7 Galerie Birkemeyer
MAP B5 ▪ 169–171 rue Mohammed El Bekal ▪ 0524 44 69 63 ▪ Open 8:30am–12:30pm & 3–7:30pm Mon–Sat, 9am–12:30pm Sun ▪ AmEx, MC, V accepted
▪ www.galerie-birkemeyer.com
Great for leather goods as well as international designer sportswear.

8 L'Orientaliste
MAP B5 ▪ 11 & 15 rue de la Liberté ▪ 0524 43 40 74 ▪ Open 9am–12:30pm & 3–7:30pm Mon–Sat, 10am–12:30pm Sun ▪ MC, V accepted
A small shop with interesting items such as tea glasses, jewellery and antique furniture.

9 Atika Chaussures
MAP B5 ▪ 34 rue de la Liberté, Guéliz ▪ 0524 43 64 09 ▪ Closed Sun
▪ Credit cards accepted
Moccasins and loafers in myriad colours adorn this fashionable store.

10 Scènes du Lin
MAP B5 ▪ 70 rue de la Liberté
▪ 0524 43 61 08 ▪ Closed Sun ▪ MC, V accepted ▪ www.scenesdelin.com
Browse through finely designed curtains with Fès embroidery and a selection of unusual lamps.

Places to Eat

PRICE CATEGORIES

For a full meal for one with half a bottle of wine (or equivalent meal), plus taxes and extra charges.

(Dh) under 200 Dh (Dh)(Dh) 200–400 Dh
(Dh)(Dh)(Dh) over 400 Dh

1 Amal

MAP B4 ■ Rue Allal Ben Ahmed, Guéliz ■ 0524 44 68 96 ■ Open 8:30am–12:30pm & noon–3:30pm daily ■ No credit cards ■ (Dh)
Dine in and support a deserving cause (see p61). Cooking classes available.

2 Grand Café de la Poste
MAP B5 ■ Cnr blvd El Mansour Eddahbi & ave Imam Malik ■ 0524 43 30 38 ■ Open 8am–1am daily ■ Credit cards accepted ■ (Dh)(Dh)
The Art Deco interior of this café, built in 1925, is largely intact. The service can be patchy.

3 +61

MAP B5 ■ 96 rue Mohammed el Beqal ■ 0524 20 70 20 ■ Open noon–4pm & 6–11pm Mon–Sat ■ Credit cards accepted ■ (Dh)(Dh)
A cosy restaurant offering Moroccan fare, as well as pasta and pizza.

4 La Trattoria Marrakech
MAP B5 ■ 179 rue Mohammed El Bekal ■ 0524 43 26 41 ■ Open noon–3pm & 7pm–midnight daily ■ MC, V accepted ■ (Dh)(Dh)
The city's best Italian restaurant is housed in a beautiful villa with seats beside the pool.

5 Comptoir Darna
MAP C6 ■ Ave Echouhada ■ 0524 43 77 02 ■ Open 7:30pm–1am daily ■ MC, V accepted ■ (Dh)(Dh)
As well as the good food, Comptoir Darna (see p56) is a great venue for night out.

6 L'Annexe

MAP B4 ■ 14 rue Moulay Ali, Guéliz ■ 0524 43 40 10 ■ Open noon–2:30pm & 7:30–11:30pm daily; closed Sat for lunch and Sun evening ■ (Dh)(Dh)
Serving perfectly executed French classics in a stylish modern bistro.

7 Al Fassia
MAP B5 ■ 55 blvd Mohammed Zerktouni ■ 0524 43 40 60 ■ Open noon–2:30pm & 7:30–11pm Wed–Mon ■ Credit cards accepted ■ (Dh)(Dh)
An excellent frill-free restaurant (see p60) with a lovely, peaceful garden.

8 Le Catanzaro
MAP B5 ■ 42 rue Tarik Bnou Ziad, Guéliz ■ 0524 43 37 31 ■ Open noon–2:30pm & 7:15–11pm Mon–Sat ■ Credit cards accepted ■ (Dh)
Reliable French/Italian restaurant serving pizzas, pastas and steaks.

9 Café Les Négociants
MAP B5 ■ Cnr ave Mohammed V & blvd Mohammed Zerktouni ■ 0524 42 23 45 ■ Open 7am–11pm daily ■ No credit cards ■ (Dh)
Stop at this popular café for a sip of strong, tar-like coffee.

10 MY Kechmara
MAP B5 ■ 3 rue de la Liberté ■ 0524 42 25 32 ■ Open 9am–midnight Mon–Sat, 9am–5pm Sun ■ MC, V accepted ■ (Dh)(Dh)
This hip bar-restaurant (see p56) wouldn't look out of place in Paris.

Stylish dining room at MY Kechmara

See map on p78

TOP 10 Essaouira

Where Marrakech is a uniform pink, this sun-beaten town, two hours and 30 minutes away on Morocco's Atlantic coast, is

a nautical blue and white. The prosperity of the place peaked in the 18th and 19th centuries when it was the most important port on the North African coast. It faded from consciousness in the 20th century, but drew plenty of travelling hippies in the 1960s and early 1970s. Today, its agreeably languid atmosphere is stirred only in late afternoon when the fishing fleet returns. Essaouira is known as the "Windy City" because of the constant winds that blow from the sea.

A cannon on Essaouira's ramparts

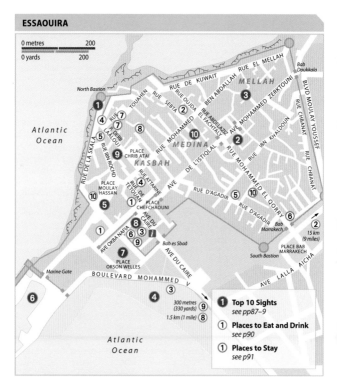

1 Top 10 Sights
see pp87–9

1 Places to Eat and Drink
see p90

1 Places to Stay
see p91

Previous pages Cacti in the Majorelle Gardens

1 Ramparts
MAP N1

Essaouira's current layout can be traced back to 1765. That year, the town's local ruler captured a French ship and hired one of its passengers, who was an architect, to rebuild his port. He had the city surrounded with a heavy defensive wall, much of which still stands today. The most impressive stretch is the Skala de la Ville, where you can go for a walk along the top of

Street sellers in the Jewish quarter, the Mellah

the ramparts and examine several of the ancient cannons in the area.

2 The Souks
MAP P1

At the heart of the medina is a lively market, the Souk Jdid, divided into four quarters by the intersection of two main thoroughfares. There is a daily souk for fish, spice and grains, and a cloistered square, known as the Joutia, where second-hand items are sold at auction.

3 The Mellah
MAP Q1

During the 18th and 19th centuries, a Jewish community gained prominence in Essaouira, becoming the most important economic group. The community has long since left and the town's Jewish quarter, or *mellah*, is in a dilapidated state. Visitors can reach it by following the alleys just inside the ramparts beyond Skala de la Ville. Former Jewish residences are fronted by balconies. In some cases, the Hebrew inscriptions on their lintels are also visible.

4 The Beach
MAP P2

Essaouira's beach, to the south of the medina, is one of the finest in Morocco. However, the strong winds that batter this part of the Atlantic coast can make it a little cold – not that this bothers the windsurfers or the boys who play football here.

5 Place Moulay Hassan
MAP N2

Place Moulay Hassan is the focal point of Essaouira. A square in two parts, narrow and elongated to the north and opening out at the southern end, it lies between the medina proper and the port, and everybody passes through it at some point. It is lined by small cafés where locals spend their time.

Ceramics for sale in the souk

Small fishing boats moored below the fortress guarding Essaouira's port

 The Port
MAP N2

Guarded by a small square fortress, Essaouira's port, the Skala du Port, is still a working concern complete with a boat yard. Even today, vessels are constructed out of wood. A daily market kicks into life between 3 and 5pm with the arrival of the day's catch. Visitors can watch as the fish are auctioned off and sample the fresh produce by indulging in the sardines that are grilled to order at the port end of place Moulay Hassan.

 Place Orson Welles
MAP N2–P2

Between the medina walls and the beach is a small park-like square named place Orson Welles, in honour of the great film-maker who travelled to Essaouira in 1949 to shoot his version of *Othello*. Since then, Essaouira and the surrounding area have been used as movie locations in many international film

Bust of the director in place Orson Welles

projects, including Oliver Stone's epic *Alexander* and Ridley Scott's *Kingdom of Heaven*.

8 Galerie Damgaard
MAP P2 ■ Ave Okba Bin Nafia, Medina ■ 0524 78 44 46 ■ Open 9am–1pm & 3–7pm daily

For about a quarter of a century a generation of painters and sculptors have made Essaouira an important centre of artistic activity. Many of these artists were brought to public attention by Dane Frederic Damgaard who used to run this influential gallery.

9 Musée Sidi Mohamed Ben Abdellah
MAP N1 ■ Rue derb Laâlouj, Medina ■ 0524 47 53 00 ■ Open 8:30am–6:30pm Wed–Mon

This small ethnographic museum occupies a 19th-century house that was formerly the town hall. It contains displays of ancient crafts, weapons and jewellery. Also displayed here are the musical instruments and accessories that were used by religious brotherhoods. You can also view some stunning examples of traditional Amazigh and Jewish costumes.

⑩ The Medina
MAP P1

As in Marrakech, Essaouira's medina is a labyrinth of narrow streets. However, it is not as hard to navigate as it is bisected by one long, straight street. This street begins at the port and runs all the way up to the north gate, the Bab Doukkala, undergoing two name changes along the way.

A narrow street of the medina

MUSIC CITY

In the late 1960s, Essaouira was a popular hippy stop-over. American singer Jimi Hendrix famously passed through, as did musician Frank Zappa and singer Cat Stevens (now known as Yusuf). The hippy influence lingers on: the annual Gnawa Festival d'Essaouira attracts many musicians from around the globe and has been described as the world's biggest jam session.

A DAY BY THE SEA

▶ **MORNING**

It is possible to do Essaouira as a day trip from Marrakech (although it's worth staying at least a couple of days). You can get an early morning **CTM** bus *(see p107)*, a Supratours coach *(see p107)* at 7:45am or a *grand taxi* from a rank behind the bus station and arrive by 10 or 11am. You will probably enter the city from the Bab Marrakech and follow rue Mohammed El Qorry to the main crossroads of the medina, which is also the middle of the **souks** *(see p87)*. Walk south down avenue de L'Istiqlal, taking a right turn into shop-lined rue Attarine. The first left leads down to **Place Moulay Hassan** *(see p87)*, a great place for a drink at one of the many cafés such as Café Bachir. Follow the road south to the port where you can have lunch.

AFTERNOON

From the port, backtrack to place Moulay Hassan but take a left at the famed **Taros** café *(see p90)* and follow the narrow alley, rue de la Skala, along the inside of the high sea wall. There are some woodcarving workshops here. After a short walk, head up to the **ramparts** *(see p87)* for a wonderful view. Descend and then continue to the *mellah (see p87)*. Find your way back to the souks and again head along avenue de L'Istiqlal south. Take a left on avenue du Caire, exiting by the Bab Es Sbaâ and taking a right for the **beach** *(see p87)*. Le Chalet de la Plage *(see p90)* is perfect for dinner by the ocean.

See map on p86

Places to Eat

PRICE CATEGORIES
For a full meal for one with half a bottle
of wine (or equivalent meal), plus taxes
and extra charges.
Ⓓ under 200 Dh   ⒹⒹ 200–400 Dh
ⒹⒹⒹ over 400 Dh

1 Port-Side Fish Stalls

MAP N2 ▪ Place Moulay Hassan
▪ Ⓓ

The best meal in Essaouira is
seafood fresh off the boat, grilled
and eaten at a group of stalls on the
port side of place Moulay Hassan.

2 La Fromagerie
Douar Larabe, Route Côtière
de Safi ▪ 0666 23 35 34 ▪ Open noon–
midnight daily ▪ ⒹⒹ

Located just a ten-minute taxi ride
from the medina. La Fromagerie is
a small hillside restaurant. Each dish
offered here involves cheese and is
made on the premises.

3 Le Chalet de la Plage
MAP P3 ▪ Blvd Mohammed V
▪ 0524 47 59 72 ▪ Open noon–
2:30pm & 6:30–10:30pm ▪ ⒹⒹ

Enjoy the superb beachfront setting
that matches the quality of fresh fish
and seafood at Le Chalet de la Plage.

4 Les Alizés Mogador
MAP N1 ▪ 26 rue de la Skala
▪ 0524 47 68 19 ▪ Open noon–
3:30pm & 7:30–11pm daily ▪ Ⓓ

This restaurant serves hearty
portions of Moroccan food.

5 Umia
MAP N2 ▪ 22 rue de la Skala
▪ 0524 78 33 95 ▪ Open 7pm–
midnight Wed–Mon ▪ ⒹⒹ

Sample lobster ravioli and chocolate
fondant at this French restaurant.

6 La Table Madada
MAP P2 ▪ Rue Youssef El Fassi
▪ 0524 47 21 06 ▪ Open 7–10pm
Wed–Mon ▪ ⒹⒹⒹ

The Madada riad is one of the cosiest
spots in town. The contemporary

See map on p86

Moroccan menu focuses on fresh
fish and Atlantic seafood alongside
produce from the market.

7 Triskala Café
MAP N1 ▪ Rue Touahen
▪ 0643 40 55 49 ▪ Open 12:30–
3:30pm & 6:30–10pm daily ▪ Ⓓ

A daily-changing menu of fresh fish,
vegetarian and vegan dishes served
in cave-like rooms just inside the
city's seafront ramparts.

8 Zahra's Grill
MAP N2 ▪ Rue Amira Lalla
Meriem ▪ 0661 90 57 22 ▪ Open
1–3pm & 7–9:30pm daily; closed
mid-Nov–mid-Mar ▪ ⒹⒹ

Expect fabulous seafood, from the
octopus salad to the lobster risotto.

9 Côté Plage
MAP Q3 ▪ Blvd Mohammed V
▪ 0524 47 90 00 ▪ ⒹⒹ

Part of the MBeach Sofitel complex,
this beachfront café serves tapas and
flavoursome barbecued meats.

10 Taros
MAP N2 ▪ Place Moulay Hassan
▪ 0524 47 64 07 ▪ Open 10am–
midnight Mon–Sat ▪ Credit cards
accepted ▪ ⒹⒹ

Enjoy the mix of Moroccan and
French dishes at Taros. There is
live music here most nights.

Taros roof terrace

Places to Stay

A peaceful and verdant courtyard at boutique hotel Villa Maroc

1 Villa Maroc

MAP P2 ■ 10 rue Abdellah Ben Yassine ■ 0524 47 31 47 ■ www.villa-maroc.com ■

Essaouira's first boutique hotel comprises four houses. It has a pool and fine views from the roof terraces.

2 Riad Dar Maya

MAP P1 ■ Rue d'Oujda ■ 0524 78 56 87 ■ www.riaddarmaya.com ■

A five-room, English-owned boutique riad with a heated rooftop plunge pool; it also has a pretty *hammam*.

3 Palazzo Desdemona

MAP P2 ■ 12–14 rue Youssef El Fassi ■ 0524 47 22 27 ■ www.palazzodesdemona.com ■

Room sizes vary but it has plenty of atmosphere and is excellent value.

4 Riad Al Madina

MAP P2 ■ 9 rue Attarine ■ 0524 47 59 07 ■ www.riadalmadina.com ■

This former hippy café, supposedly frequented by Jimi Hendrix, has been restored as a charming riad.

5 Riad Nakhla

MAP P2 ■ 12 rue d'Agadir ■ 0524 47 52 30 ■ www.riadnakhla.com ■

All rooms have en-suite bathrooms; there's a courtyard with a fountain and a terrific roof terrace.

6 Heure Bleue Palais

MAP Q2 ■ 2 rue Ibn Batouta ■ 0524 78 34 34 ■ www.heure-bleue.com ■

This Relais & Chateaux member has luxe rooms, a rooftop pool and a spa, and offers superb fine dining.

7 Dar Adul

MAP N1 ■ 63 rue Touahen ■ 0524 47 39 10 ■

A cosy house with seven bedrooms, a sitting room and a roof terrace.

8 Riad Malaïka

MAP P1 ■ Rue Zayan ■ 0524 78 49 08 ■ www.riad-essaouira-malaika.com ■

Beautifully preserved 300-year-old riad. Rooms are small but nicely decorated. It also has a roof terrace.

9 Madada Mogador

MAP P2 ■ Rue Youssef El Fassi ■ 0524 47 55 12 ■ Open 11:30am–2pm & 6–10:30pm daily ■ www.madada.com ■

Perfectly located overlooking place Orson Welles and the beach; with spacious rooms and a roof terrace.

10 Lalla Mira

MAP Q2 ■ 14 rue d'Algérie ■ 0634 94 97 71 ■

Located near the souks, this simple riad, with friendly staff, features brightly coloured rooms and a roof terrace with stunning views.

🔟 Tizi-n-Test Pass

The high-altitude Tizi-n-Test Pass, the more westerly of the two great passes over the Atlas Mountains, is cautiously navigated by the R203 highway to Taroudant. Although the distance between the two cities is only 223 km (138 miles), the road's tortuous hairpins demand so much respect from drivers that the journey takes nearly five hours – not including time to stop off and take in the views along the way. Travellers without their own vehicle or *grand taxi* can make the trip by public transport: southbound buses depart Marrakech each morning. Visitors can also save time by changing buses in Agadir.

The roofless arches of Tin Mal

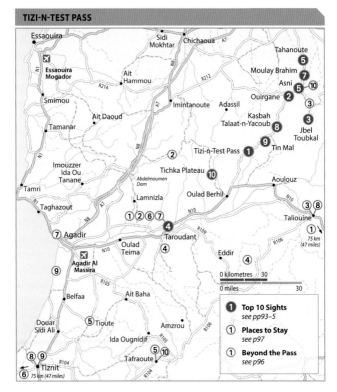

TIZI-N-TEST PASS

1 **Top 10 Sights**
see pp93–5

1 **Places to Stay**
see p97

1 **Beyond the Pass**
see p96

Snow capped Jbel Toubkal towering over palm trees in the valley below

1 Tizi-n-Test Pass
MAP B2

How much travellers enjoy the experience of this 2,092-m (6,861-ft) pass depends on whether they are a passenger or in the driver's seat. Drivers have to keep their eyes glued to the road ahead in order to negotiate the endless hairpin bends. The narrow road, with no safety barriers, means there aren't many opportunities to enjoy the beautiful views. But for those in the passenger seat, the vistas across the plains of the Sous to the south are spectacular. There are various souvenir stalls and small cafés located on the pass itself, where drivers and passengers can stop and take in the scenery.

2 Ouirgane
MAP C2

A pretty little village 16 km (10 miles) south of Asni, Ouirgane is hidden among the tree-lined valley above the Oued Nifis river. Here, there is a shrine to a Jewish saint as well as two salt factories (one modern, one traditional). The village is a great base for hiking, mountain biking or horse-riding excursions into the Atlas Mountains.

3 Jbel Toubkal
MAP C2 ■ Bureau des guides:
tel 0524 48 56 26

Take the left fork at Asni to Imlil (see p63) at the foot of Jbel Toubkal, North Africa's highest peak. Climbing Toubkal is not particularly difficult, but the fact that it is a high-altitude hike over rough terrain should be taken into account. Mountain guides can be hired in the centre of Imlil at the *bureau des guides*. The Kasbah du Toubkal (see p97), just up the hill, is a good place to stay.

4 Taroudant
MAP B2

Built on the proceeds of gold brought from the Sahara, Taroudant was the capital of the Saadian dynasty in the early 16th century. Today, enclosed within reddish-yellow walls, the city resembles a smaller, sleepier version of Marrakech. It features a grand kasbah that can be reached by passing under the triple-arched Saadian Gates, as well as some foul-smelling tanneries. You will also find two excellent souks in Taroudant.

A souk in the city of Taroudant

Country market at Tahanoute

5 Tahanoute
MAP C1

The administrative centre of Tahanoute is just a 20-minute drive south of Marrakech. The old village has a cascade of red clay houses that surround a massive rock sheltering the shrine of Sidi Mohammed El Kebir, whose festival is celebrated at Mouloud – the birthday of the Prophet Mohammed. This was the subject of Winston Churchill's last painting in 1958. A market is held here every Tuesday.

6 Asni
MAP C2

The village of Asni lies at a fork in the road – a left turn leads up to the village of Imlil and the striking kasbahs of Tamadot (see p97) and Toubkal (see p63). Jbel Toubkal dominates the view

to the west, but there is little for visitors to explore at Asni itself, apart from shops selling trinkets (although these are cheaper in Marrakech). The highlight here is the busy country market held on Saturdays – one of the largest in the Atlas Mountains.

7 Moulay Brahim
MAP C2

South of Tahanoute, the road winds uphill to Moulay Brahim, named after a local saint. There is a green-roofed shrine dedicated to him in the middle of the village which non-Muslims are forbidden to enter.

8 Kasbah Talaat-n-Yacoub
MAP C2

South of Ourigane, the road climbs steadily through a bare and rocky landscape. After you pass through the Amazigh hamlet of Ijoujak, the hilltop fortress of Kasbah Talaat-n-Yacoub is visible to the right. This was once a stronghold of the Goundafi tribe who controlled access to the Tizi-n-Test pass until the early 20th century, when they were subdued by the French.

9 Tin Mal
MAP C2 ■ Closed Fridays ■ Adm

The main attraction at Tin Mal is an ancient mosque that dates back to the time of the Almohads (see p38). Back in the 12th century, this was the heart

The hillside town of Asni

ARGAN OIL

The precious argan trees, similar in appearance to olive trees, are found only in southwest Morocco. They bear a fruit from which oil can be extracted by splitting, roasting and pressing the nuts. Locals use it as a medicine; it is also a staple of beauty and massage treatments, and tastes delicious when drizzled on couscous.

of a mountain empire that unified local tribes under a militant version of Islam. It was from here that an army set out in 1144 to lay siege to Marrakech and went on to conquer the rest of Morocco. The restored mosque provided the basic architectural prototype for the impressive Koutoubia in Marrakech. Though roofless, it continues to be the venue for Friday prayers – the only day that it is inaccessible to non-Muslim visitors.

10 Tichka Plateau
MAP B2

Set among beautiful meadows, the Tichka Plateau is found to the north of Taroudant. Particularly striking in spring, when the wild flowers are in full bloom, it is a fine place to go trekking, but is best enjoyed with qualified guides. Go to the *bureau des guides* in Imlil (see p93) to arrange a guided trek.

A DAY IN TAROUDANT

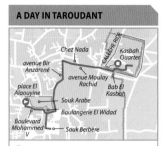

▶ **MORNING**

Although **Taroudant** (see p93) resembles a more ramshackle Marrakech at first sight, it has more of an African identity than an Arab one. Unlike most other Moroccan cities, it was never occupied by the French and it does not possess a European quarter. Begin your exploration of the city on place El Alaouyine, known by its Amazigh name of place Assarag. Walk down boulevard Mohammed V, south of the square, and head east into Souk Arabe, famed for its antique shops. At the souk's edge, **Boulangerie El Widad** (+212 5288 52150) on boulevard Mohammed V, offers tasty Moroccan pastries. South of the main street and across place El Nasr is Souk Berbère, the main fruit and vegetable market. Return north up avenue Bir Anzarené and take a right; sample the tajines at **Chez Nada** (15 avenue Moulay Rachid).

AFTERNOON

As you walk east on avenue Moulay Rachid along a path lined with orange trees, you will come upon the triple-arched Saadian Gates at Bab El Kasbah. These lead to the walled kasbah quarter built by Mohammed ech-Cheikh, who made it the capital of the Saadian empire. The poorest part of town, it used to house the governor's palace. Stop for a snack at one of the local cafés and then make your way back to the Bab El Kasbah. Hop into a taxi and head back to place El Alaouyine.

See map on p92 ←

Beyond the Pass

 Taznakht
MAP C2

Famed for the carpets woven by the Ouaouzgite tribe, the town of Taznakht sits beneath Jbel Siroua.

2 The Atlas Mountains
MAP B2

The peaks of the western High Atlas – particularly 3,555-m (11,667-ft) high Jbel Aoulime – can be reached by road north of Taroudant.

3 Taliouine
MAP C2

Taliouine, a town with a ruined kasbah once owned by the Glaoui clan *(see p100)*, is also one of the world's biggest saffron-growing areas.

 The Anti-Atlas
MAP C3

As the R106 from Taliouine crosses the Anti-Atlas at the 94-km (58-mile) mark, you'll find Igherm – a large mountain village where women wear black with coloured headbands.

The impressive Tioute Kasbah

5 Tioute Kasbah
MAP B3

About 37 km (23 miles) southeast of Taroudant, the imposing Tioute Kasbah (containing a restaurant) dominates a palm grove. This was the location for the film *Ali Baba and the Forty Thieves* in 1954.

A colourful building in Sidi Ifni

6 Sidi Ifni

This colonial-style town sits on the crest of a rocky plateau over-looking the Atlantic. To get here, follow the coast road after Tiznit.

 7 Agadir
MAP A3 ■ Tourist information: ave du Prince Moulay Abdallah ■ 0528 84 63 77

Flattened by an earthquake in 1960, Agadir was rebuilt and is now a thriving charter tourist resort. The grim aspect of the town is somewhat offset by its fantastic beaches.

 8 Tiznit
MAP A3

In this small town, surrounded by pink *pisé* ramparts, visitors feel the proximity of both the Atlantic and the desert. Its central *méchouar* parade ground is lined with cafés and shops.

9 Souss Massa National Park
MAP A3

The park along the banks of Wadi Massa contains reed beds inhabited by large flocks of flamingoes and the endangered northern bald ibis.

10 Tafraoute
MAP B3

At an altitude of 1,200 m (3,938 ft), Tafraoute stands in the heart of a stunning valley in the Anti-Atlas. The palm groves here are lush and when they flower in February, the almond trees are covered with clouds of dusky pink and white blossom.

→ *See map on p92*

Places to Stay

PRICE CATEGORIES

For a standard double room per night with taxes and breakfast if included.

Dh under 1,200 Dh   Dh Dh 1,200–2,500 Dh
Dh Dh Dh over 2,500 Dh

1 Le Palais Oumensour
MAP B2 ▪ Burj Al Mansour Oumensour Tadjount, Taroudant ▪ 0528 55 02 15 ▪ www.palaisoumensour.com ▪ No credit cards ▪ Dh

Well located for those who wish to explore Taroudant on foot, this hotel has stylish, comfortable rooms.

2 Hotel Dar Zitoune
MAP B2 ▪ Boutarial El Barrania, Taroudant ▪ 0528 55 11 42 ▪ www.darzitoune.ma ▪ Dh Dh

Set out like an Amazigh village, this riad features a large pool and offers suites, bungalows and tented rooms.

3 Kasbah du Toubkal
MAP C2 ▪ BP31, Imlil ▪ 0524 48 56 11 ▪ www.kasbahdutoubkal.com ▪ Dh Dh

This beautifully restored kasbah is a great base for trekking (see p63).

4 Riad Ain Khadra
MAP B2 ▪ Route d'Agadir, Taroudant ▪ 0528 85 41 42 ▪ No credit cards ▪ www.riad-ain-khadra.com ▪ Dh

The French owners of this charming maison d'hôtes have five traditional rooms and three suites arranged around a courtyard pool.

5 L'Arganier d'Ammelne
MAP B3 ▪ Route d'Agadir, Tafraoute ▪ 0661 92 60 64 ▪ www.arganierammelne.jimdo.com ▪ Dh

A few minutes' drive from central Tafraout, this basic but comfortable option has air-conditioned en-suite rooms, a garden and a terrace. It also offers camping options.

6 Domaine Villa Talaa
MAP B2 ▪ Taroudant ▪ 0676 64 77 94 ▪ Dh

About a ten-minute drive from Taroudant is this peaceful hotel with 11 rooms. All have patios opening onto the garden and the pool.

7 Dar Fatima
MAP B2 ▪ Tasoukt Ighzifn, Taroudant ▪ 0661 60 66 22 ▪ www.darfatima.com ▪ Dh

Right in the centre of town, this simple yet friendly riad has great views from its rooftop terrace.

8 Escale Rando Taliouine
MAP C2 ▪ Taliouine ▪ 0528 53 46 00 ▪ www.escalerando.com ▪ Dh

This sparse but functional hotel occupies part of an old kasbah. The hospitable owners are happy to arrange treks and tours.

9 Hotel Idou Tiznit
MAP A3 ▪ Ave Hassan II, Tiznit ▪ 0528 60 03 33 ▪ Credit cards accepted ▪ Dh

Notable for its location, this hotel is a good option for those travelling on a limited budget.

10 Kasbah Tamadot
MAP C2 ▪ BP67, Asni ▪ 0524 36 82 00 ▪ www.virginlimitededition.com/kasbah-tamadot ▪ Dh Dh Dh

Owned by Richard Branson, this expensive retreat is located in a tranquil spot at the foothills of the Atlas Mountains.

A suite at Kasbah Tamadot

TOP 10 Tizi-n-Tichka Pass

Intricate stucco, Kasbah Telouet

The N9 highway runs southeast from Marrakech over the Atlas Mountains, crossing the country's highest pass. On the other side, it then descends to the town of Ouarzazate, considered the gateway to the Sahara. Along the way, travellers will come across some interesting sights, including the kasbahs of Telouet and Aït Benhaddou (both off the main road). From start to finish, the route is 196 km (122 miles) on a good road. There are some stretches that demand careful driving; as a result, the journey can take nearly four hours. Travellers can arrange for a *grand taxi* or hire a car. Alternatively, several buses travel this route daily from Marrakech's bus station. Transport company Supratours also runs daily trips to Ouarzazate.

1 Tizi-n-Tichka Pass
MAP C2

As the road leaves Taddert, the green landscape turns scenically rugged and barren – the twisting, precipitous drops keeping drivers focused. At its highest point, the pass peaks at 2,260 m (7,415 ft), marked by no more than a few stalls selling colourful rocks found in the region.

While some of these rocks are fake, the real ones reveal glittering crystal formations when broken.

2 Aït Ourir
MAP C1

This busy rural town 35 km (22 miles) outside Marrakech becomes more active on Fridays, when farmers trade camels, sheep and other

TIZI-N-TICHKA PASS

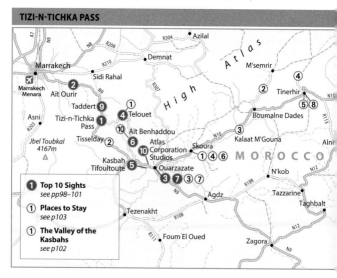

1 **Top 10 Sights**
see pp98–101

1 **Places to Stay**
see p103

1 **The Valley of the Kasbahs**
see p102

The winding road that forms the Tizi-n-Tichka Pass

other agricultural produce in a weekly country market. If visitors pass through on the right day, it makes for a great hour-long stop off.

3 Kasbah Taourirt
MAP D2 ▪ Open 8am–5pm daily ▪ Adm

The main landmark of Ouarzazate, this large kasbah used to belong to the Glaoui tribe. Parts are still inhabited, while other sections have been carefully restored. Its atmospheric,

narrow alleys evoke a sense of what life here was like in the 19th century.

4 Kasbah Telouet
MAP C2 ▪ Adm

Telouet, the stronghold of the Glaoui tribe (see p100), who, in the early 20th century, came to rule all of southern Morocco under French sponsorship, is a village dominated by a kasbah. Abandoned for nearly half a century, much of the structure is crumbling and dangerous. However, you can visit the ornate reception hall and its rooftop terrace, which offers great views.

5 Kasbah Tifoultoute
MAP D2 ▪ Open 8am–5pm daily

Tifoultoute is another kasbah that once belonged to the Glaoui, and is situated just outside of Ouarzazate. Although parts of it are crumbling away, one section has been rebuilt and serves as a hotel and restaurant.

The magnificent Kasbah Tifoultoute

THAMI EL GLAOUI

In 1893, the Glaoui tribe of Telouet was rewarded for rescuing Sultan Moulay Hassan and his army from a raging blizzard. They benefited further after the French took over – Thami El Glaoui was made *pasha* (lord) and became one of the most powerful men in the country. Hated for his support of the French, he died soon after Morocco gained independence in 1956.

The town of Ouarzazate

Aït Benhaddou
MAP D2

This sprawling kasbah features on UNESCO's list of World Heritage Sites and is one of the best pre-served in the region. It is also among the most famous, and, thanks to its popularity with visiting film pro-ducers and directors, it has been immortalized in dozens of Hollywood movies, including *Lawrence of Arabia*, *The Last Temptation of Christ*, *The Mummy*, *Gladiator* and *Alexander*. Part of its appeal lies in its location, with the kasbah tumbling down a hillside beside the Ouarzazate River. It is still partially inhabited by a few families.

Ouarzazate
MAP D2 ■ Tourist Office: 0524 88 23 66

The so-called "Gateway to the Sahara" (pronounced "war-zazat") is a town of around 60,000 people. Most visitors tend to spend at least one night here before pushing on south to the desert proper, or heading east to the Dadès Gorge and beyond *(see p102)*. The number of hotels in town is always increasing and the quality is constantly improving. There are plenty of interesting activities in the area: from camel-trekking and quad biking to desert safaris and guided tours of the Atlas film studios for which the town is renowned.

Aït Benhaddou

8 Valley of the Kasbahs

From Ouarzazate, visitors can continue east through the Skoura Valley along a road dotted with oases and the ancient mud-brick strongholds that give the route its more romantic nickname *(see p102)*. The road eventually runs out at Merzouga, 350 miles (562 km) from Marrakech, and there is nothing to be found between here and the Algerian border but sand dunes.

9 Taddert
MAP C1

After Aït Ourir, the last stop before the pass is the busy village of Taddert. In the higher part of the settlement, a handful of good cafés offer views of the valley below. When the pass is closed by bad weather, a barrier is lowered to halt all traffic.

The lush valley below Taddert

10 Atlas Corporation Studios
MAP D2 ▪ 0524 88 22 12 ▪ Open 8:15am–6:45pm daily ▪ Guided tours last 30–40 mins ▪ Adm

Ouarzazate has become the centre of the Moroccan film industry and is home to the Atlas Corporation Studios. Found 6 km (4 miles) to the north of town, the studios were built to provide infrastructure, sound stages and sets for movies; films shot here include *Gladiator* and *Kingdom of Heaven*, as well as episodes of the world-famous *Game of Thrones*. Film buffs can see sets here such as the Egyptian temple from the French production of *Asterix and Cleopatra*. A shuttle bus runs between the studio and avenue Mohammed V.

SOUTH TO THE DESERT

▶ DAY ONE

From **Ouarzazate**, the road continues south through the Drâa Valley down to the administrative town of Zagora. After a drive of about four hours, stop at Tamnougalt, a dramatic *ksar* (fortified village) 10 minutes off the main road, 5 km (3 miles) after the small market town of Agdz. Further south is Kasbah Timiderte, a fortress from the Glaoui era. Zagora itself is dominated by Jbel Zagora, a rocky outcrop at the town's end. The lively market, held on Wednesdays and Sundays, teems with dates that grow in abundance here. Just south of the centre is the pretty hamlet of Amezrou. Nearby, the Kasbah des Juifs is inhabited by Amazigh silversmiths (the Jews who once lived here are long gone). Zagora's most famous attraction is at the town's exit – a sign with a camel caravan that reads "Timbuktu, 52 Days".

DAY TWO

The village of M'Hamid is 96 km (60 miles) further south of Zagora. En route, Tamegroute's mosque-and-shrine complex is off limits to non-Muslims, except for the library with its collection of ancient manuscripts. Drive 5 km (3 miles) further on and you will see the first of the Tinfou Dunes. The best dunes can be accessed from M'Hamid, a sleepy outpost at the road's end – a one-street settlement that feels like it is at the end of the world. Desert trips, from excursions of a few hours, to expeditions lasting several days, can be arranged.

See map on pp98–9

The Valley of the Kasbahs

 Skoura
MAP D2

The first town east of Ouarzazate is notable for a *palmeraie* with impressive old kasbahs including the Kasbah Amridil (part hotel, part museum), once owned by the Glaoui family *(see p100)*.

Kasbah Amridil, near Skoura

 Dadès Gorge
MAP E1

Follow the road north from Boumalne Dades to this incredible gorge, a spectacular backdrop for several kasbahs.

③ Kalaat M'Gouna
MAP D2

This small town lies at the heart of rose-growing country. Most of the petals picked each spring are exported around the world for use in the perfume industry.

④ Todra Gorge
MAP E1

Sheer cliffs rise from this narrow gorge with Tamtattouchte village at the northern end. Two hotels make an overnight stay possible.

Erg Chebbi dunes, Merzouga

 Tinerhir
MAP E1 ■ **Tourist information:**
Hotel Tombouctou; 0524 83 51 91

The region's administrative centre is bordered by lush palm groves. Known for its silver jewellery, it has several working silver mines nearby.

⑥ Goulmima
MAP E1

The fortified villages, or *ksours*, here were built to defend against the pillaging nomads. A walled town east of the Erfoud road is worth a detour.

⑦ Errachidia
MAP F1 ■ **Tourist information:**
0535 57 09 44

From this town, known for its pottery and carved wooden objects, the palm groves of Ziz and Tafilalt begin.

 Erfoud
MAP F1

This town serves as a base for tours to the Erg Chebbi sand dunes and the Tafilalt palm grove. It also hosts a three-day Date Festival each October following the date harvest.

⑨ Rissani
MAP F1

This ancient town dating back to the 7th century lies on the edge of the Sahara and has a very famous souk.

 Merzouga
MAP F2

A Saharan oasis at the foot of the Erg Chebbi dunes, from where camel drivers offer desert tours.

Places to Stay

① Auberge Telouet
MAP C2 ▪ Telouet ▪ 0524 89 07 17 ▪ www.telouet.com ▪ No credit cards ▪ Ⓓⓗ

A lovely budget auberge in the traditional style. The walls are made of huge stones, and rooms are spartan but attractive. Not all rooms have en-suite facilities.

② Irocha
MAP C2 ▪ Tisselday ▪ 0667 73 70 02 ▪ www.irocha.com ▪ No credit cards ▪ Ⓓⓗ

Midway between Telouet and Aït Benhaddou, this hotel has plenty of charming touches, such as multiple terraces and gardens. It also has a pool and a *hammam*.

③ Le Berbère Palace
MAP D2 ▪ Quartier Mansour Eddahabi Ouarzazate ▪ 0524 88 31 05 ▪ www.hotel-berberepalace.com ▪ ⒹⓗⒹⓗ

One of the three luxury hotels in Ouarzazate, it has air-conditioned bungalows, a large pool, a *hammam*, a solarium and tennis courts.

④ Kasbah Aït Ben Moro
MAP D2 ▪ Skoura ▪ 0524 85 21 16 ▪ www.kasbahaitbenmoro.com ▪ No credit cards ▪ Ⓓⓗ

At night, this 18th-century fortress with thick walls and a palm-tree garden is lit by lanterns, creating a cosy atmosphere.

⑤ Riad Salam
MAP F1 ▪ Route de Rissani, Erfoud ▪ 0535 57 66 65 ▪ www.hotel-erfoud-riad.com ▪ Ⓓⓗ

While this is a budget option, it has plenty to offer, including a swimming pool and a popular bar.

⑥ Dar Ahlam
MAP D2 ▪ Douar Oulad, Chakh Ali, Skoura ▪ 0524 85 22 39 ▪ www.darahlam.com ▪ ⒹⓗⒹⓗⒹⓗ

A kasbah-turned-luxury-boutique hotel with a *hammam*, candle-lit massage room and swimming pool.

⑦ Dar Daïf
MAP D2 ▪ Route de Zagora, Ouarzazate ▪ 0524 85 49 47 ▪ www.dardaif.ma ▪ Ⓓⓗ

This 15-room guesthouse has a *hammam*, a pool and a bedroom equipped for disabled guests.

Dar Daïf's courtyard and pool

⑧ Kasbah Lamrani
MAP E1 ▪ Zone Touristique, blvd Mohammed V, Tinerhir ▪ 0524 83 50 17 ▪ www.kasbahlamrani.com ▪ Ⓓⓗ

This small kasbah, with a pool, is a good base for a trip to the Todra Gorge.

⑨ Kasbah Xaluca
MAP F1 ▪ Erfoud ▪ 0535 57 84 50 ▪ www.xaluca.com ▪ Ⓓⓗ

A large place with a big swimming pool, this is tailored to suit groups.

⑩ La Rose du Sable
MAP D2 ▪ Aït Benhaddou ▪ 0524 89 00 22 ▪ www.larose dusable.com ▪ Ⓓⓗ

Very comfortable, family-friendly hotel with a courtyard swimming pool and great views of the kasbah.

See map on pp98–9

Streetsmart

Moroccan spices in colourful
tajines at the Spice Market

Getting Around

Arriving by Air

Marrakech is served by **Marrakech Airport** (RAK), which is just 3 miles (5 km) from the Medina. The national carrier **Royal Air Maroc** is the main domestic airline and also offers regular international services. The cheapest flights tend to be those operated by the budget companies such as **easyJet**, **Ryanair** and **Norwegian**. Many major European airlines, as well as **Etihad** and **Qatar Airways**, fly direct to Marrakech. Other international airlines may fly into Casablanca, requiring a change of carrier, or require connections via a European hub, such as Paris or Madrid.

On arrival you need to complete an embarkation card before passport control. Once you have collected your luggage, taxis can be found outside the arrivals hall. Prices for airport taxis are massively inflated – head to the taxis in the car park instead. There is a board showing prices to various parts of Marrakech, however, the drivers do not usually follow it. It is advisable that you agree a price with your driver before setting off. For Jemaa el Fna or Guéliz you should not pay more than 70 Dh.

There is also a bus (No 19), which departs every 20–30 minutes and which runs to Jemaa el Fna via all the large hotels; it costs 30 Dh, with a free return journey if taken within two weeks of departure.

Train Travel

The train network in Morocco is not extensive but the service is excellent, benefitting from substantial investment. Train services from Casablanca, Fès, Rabat and Tangier arrive at Marrakech's impressive **ONCF Railway Station**, which is located on the western edge of the new city. It has the city's only free public toilets, as well as a range of Western fast-food outlets. From the station it is a short walk into central Guéliz, or a ten-minute taxi ride to Jemaa el Fna for the Medina, which should cost no more than 50 Dh.

Bus Travel

Long-distance buses connect all major towns and cities. Both the national bus company, **CTM**, and the biggest private bus company, **Supratours**, run buses to and from Marrakech and other major Moroccan destinations. The CTM station is just south of the train station, while the Supratours ticket office is at the train station. The buses are comfortable and cheap. On busy routes, such as from Marrakech to Essaouira and from Casablanca to Marrakech, it is advisable to book the seat a few days ahead.

Taxis

Everybody gets around by taxi. There are two types: *grands taxis* and *petits taxis*. The former, which tend to be big Peugeots or Mercedes, are used for long-distance journeys (and the airport run) and operate like minibuses, collecting multiple passengers going to various destinations but all generally in the same direction. The *grand taxis* often ply routes that are not well-served by the buses, including over the Tizi-n-Test and Tizi-n-Tichka passes. Be aware that usage of seatbelts is rare and drivers often don't adhere to speed limits.

Petits taxis are standard beige-coloured cars used for short-distance journeys and carrying a maximum of three passengers. They can be flagged down on the street. These taxis often do not have meters and it is necessary to negotiate a fixed price in advance with the driver. paying more than you need to, ask at your hotel what the correct fares are for local journeys. Petits taxis are not permitted to carry passengers beyond the limits of the city in which they operate. If you want to make a daytrip out of town you need to hire a grand taxi.

Calèches

Traditional horse-drawn open carriages, or *calèches*, are used almost exclusively by tourists taking sightseeing trips around the city walls. You can find them just west of Jemaa el Fna on Place foucault. Prices are listed on a signboard.

Cycling

Marrakech was the first African city to launch a bike-sharing scheme, **Medina Bike**, which has 300 bikes and 10 stations. However, the roads can be chaotic and so nervous cyclists may prefer to take a bike tour with a guide. Further afield, the Tizi-n-Test and Tizi-n-Tichka passes are both popular climbs with road cyclists, and can be incorporated as part of a multi-day tour in the Atlas Mountains.

Walking

Marrakech is small and the best way to get around is on foot. In fact, in the Medina you have no choice, as Jemaa el Fna and many other areas are off limits to cars. This does not, however, prevent the large number of scooters and bicycles that career through the alleys, ignoring the signs forbidding such vehicles. The network of streets is labyrinthine and street signs are few so expect to get lost a lot. When you do, don't panic, because you will never be more than a few minutes' walk from somewhere familiar.

The walk to the new town of Guéliz, beyond the old city walls, takes about 20 minutes.

Travelling Outside the City

For excursions outside of Marrekech, to neighbouring cities, the countryside or perhaps over the Atlas Mountains, take a bus, taxi or car.

Grand taxis gather at the bus station *(gare routière)*, just south of the train station. These go to Casablanca, Fès and Essaouira, among other places. The fares are fixed; you just have to turn up and take a seat. Once the vehicle has filled with passengers it leaves.

Buses are slightly more expensive but more comfortable and they run to a schedule. Supratours services are superior to CTM, but the latter serves more places, including destinations south of the Atlas Mountains.

A car is by far the easiest way to explore beyond the city. A popular option is to hire your own car and driver. This gives you complete flexibility. Most hotels can organize this for you. You can also hire a car and drive yourself – international car hire companies, such as **Avis**, **Europcar**, **Hertz** and **Sixt**, are represented in Marrakech. Car hire is quite expensive, with local agencies charging around 400 Dh a day. Check the terms of your agreement carefully, especially clauses relating to insurance and cover in case of accident or theft. A four-wheel-drive car is a must for heading south over the Atlas Mountains as roads are often steep and the terrain is rocky.

The Moroccan highway code is similar to that of France, so drive on the right and give way to traffic on the right at roundabouts and junctions. Road signs are in Arabic and French.

DIRECTORY

ARRIVING BY AIR

easyJet
W easyjet.com

Etihad
W etihad.com

Marrakech Airport
C 0524 44 79 10

Norwegian
W norwegian.com

Qatar Airways
W qatarairways.com

Royal Air Maroc
W royalairmaroc.com

Ryanair
W ryanair.com

TRAIN TRAVEL

ONCF Railway Station
MAP B5
▪ Avenue Hassan II
W oncf.ma

BUS TRAVEL

CTM
MAP B5
▪ Boulevard Aboubaker Seddik
W ctm.ma

Supratours
MAP B5
▪ Avenue Hassan II
W supratours.ma

CYCLING

Medina Bike
W medinabike.ma

TRAVELLING OUTSIDE THE CITY

Avis
W avis.com

Europcar
W europcar.com

Hertz
W hertz.com

Sixt
W sixt.com

Practical Information

Passports and Visas

For entry requirements, including visas, consult your nearest Moroccan embassy or check the Moroccan **Ministry of Foreign Affairs** website. Citizens of the UK, EU, Switzerland, the United States, Canada, Australia and New Zealand need a valid passport to visit Morocco, but a visa is not required. To be able to stay for up to 90 days, your passport should be valid for at least six months post your date of arrival. If your stay exceeds 90 days, then you must get an extension from the central police station.

Government Advice

Now more than ever, it is important to consult both your and the Moroccan government's advice before travelling. The **UK Foreign and Commonwealth Office**, the **US State Department**, the **Australian Department of Foreign Affairs and Trade** and **Visit Morocco** (the national tourist board) offer the latest information on security, health and local regulations.

Customs Information

You can find information on the laws relating to goods and currency taken in or out of Morocco on the **Customs and Excise Administration** website. Visitors are permitted to bring the following into Morocco for personal use: 200 cigarettes or 400g of tobacco, 1 litre of spirits and 1 litre of wine, 150ml of perfume and 250ml of eau de toilette.

Insurance

We recommend that you take out a comprehensive insurance policy covering theft, loss of belongings, medical care, cancellations and delays, and read the small print carefully. Morocco does not have any reciprocal health care agreements with other countries, and if you fall ill you will have to pay the doctor's bills.

Health

Morocco has both a public and a private healthcare system. Generally speaking, treatment in private hospitals is of a higher standard than that given in the under-funded public sector. In case of an emergency don't wait for an ambulance. You should flag a taxi and go to the **Clinique Le Marrakech** – open 24 hours – in Targa, 8 km (5 miles) northwest of the Medina. This is a private hospital with the best treatment.

Pharmacies such as **Pharmacie Centrale** and **Pharmacie du Progrès** are denoted by a green crescent sign and have well-informed staff, who often speak English.

For information about COVID-19 vaccination requirements, consult government advice. No other vaccinations are required for visitors entering Morocco, except for those coming from a country where yellow fever exists. Vaccinations against hepatitis A and B and typhoid are advised. It is best to avoid drinking tap water; many establishments serve filtered water to limit the use of plastic bottles.

Smoking, Alcohol and Drugs

Moroccan law prohibits smoking in most public buildings but this is rarely enforced.

Although Muslims are forbidden to drink alcohol, Morocco is a moderate Islamic country. It has a few bars and most restaurants, especially those frequented by foreigners, serve beer, wine and spirits.

While hashish, known locally as *kif*, is illegal, plenty of Moroccans smoke it. Visitors may well be offered *kif* for sale, but the penalty for buying or smoking it is ten years' imprisonment. It is best avoided.

ID

Visitors to Morocco are not required to carry ID at all times, but it is a good idea to keep a photocopy of the information pages of your passport on your person just in case.

Personal Security

Violence is rare, though bag snatching and other such opportunistic crimes can occur. Pickpockets are also common in the souks and on Jemaa el Fna, so be vigilant.

Morocco is a largely Muslim country with conservative views. As such, visitors should dress modestly, particularly when travelling outside the city. In practice, this means covering the shoulders and not wearing shorts. Dresses and skirts should be at least knee length. It is not necessary to cover your hair.

Homosexuality is illegal in Morocco, and is technically punishable by up to three years of imprisonment. However, this is rarely enforced, and this law does not apply to non-Moroccan same-sex partners visiting the country. All travellers should use discretion, regardless of sexual orientation. Public displays of affection by anyone are generally frowned upon, and should be avoided.

If you do experience any problems while in Marrakech, try the tourist police – the **Brigade Touristique** – at Sidi Mimoun, to the west of Jemaa el Fna (not to be confused with the Judicial Police to the east of Jemaa el Fna), or call the **police, ambulance and fire brigade** emergency numbers. The main police station is on rue Ibn Hanbal near Jnane El Harti in the New City.

Travellers with Specific Requirements

Those with limited mobility will find Marrakech tricky to navigate, especially in the Medina where the crowded roads tend to be narrow and in poor condition. There is little adapted infrastructure such as wheelchair-friendly ramps, signs in Braille, or beeping and flashing pedestrian crossings. Beyond the large hotels and the railway station, very few buildings are disabled-friendly, though the city's better riads will do their best to accommodate. On the plus side, Moroccans are extremely accommodating and resourceful, and do their best to make things as easy as possible. The **Disabled Tourist Guide** website offers information and advice on travel in Morocco for those with specific requirements.

Time Zone

Morocco standard time follows Greenwich Mean Time (GMT).

Money

The Moroccan unit of currency is the dirham (Dh), divided into 100 centimes. Debit cards and credit cards such as Visa and MasterCard are accepted in most shops and restaurants. American Express is less widely accepted. Be aware that credit cards often attract a surcharge of 5 per cent. ATMs are widely available in Marrakech and neighbouring towns and cities. It is always worth carrying some cash, as many small businesses and markets still accept cash only.

Tipping is an ingrained part of Moroccan society. Almost any service rendered will warrant a tip, known as *baksheesh*. Keep a stash of small denomination notes for this purpose.

DIRECTORY

PASSPORTS AND VISAS

Ministry of Foreign Affairs
w consulat.ma

GOVERNMENT ADVICE

Australian Department of Foreign Affairs and Trade
w smartraveller.gov.au

UK Foreign and Commonwealth Office
w gov.uk/foreign-travel-advice

US State Department
w travel.state.gov

Visit Morocco
w visitmorocco.com

CUSTOMS INFORMATION

Customs and Excise Administration
w douane.gov.ma

HEALTH

Clinique le Marrakech
Quartier Masmoudi Targa
w cliniquelemarrakech.ma

Pharmacie Centrale
MAP B5 ■ 166 ave Mohammed V, Guéliz
c 0524 43 01 58

Pharmacie du Progrès
MAP J3 ■ Jemaa el Fna
c 0524 44 25 63

PERSONAL SECURITY

Ambulance and Fire Brigade
c 150

Brigade Touristique
c 0524 38 46 01

Police
c 19

TRAVELLERS WITH SPECIFIC REQUIREMENTS

Disabled Tourist Guide
w disabled-tourist-guide.com

Electrical Appliances

The electric current is 220V/50Hz. Moroccan sockets take European-style two-pin plugs.

Mobile Phones and Wi-Fi

The national operator Maroc-Télécom and rivals Meditél and INWI have arrangements with European networks that allow visitors to use their home mobile networks in Morocco. If you are visiting for a long period, it is advisable to buy a pre-paid SIM card from any of the operators, with shops just off place du 16 Novembre in the New City.

Free Wi-Fi is common throughout Marrakech. Many hotels and riads offer free Wi-Fi, as do many cafés and train or bus stations.

Postal Services

There is a main post office on the south side of Jemaa el Fna, which opens 8am–8pm Monday to Friday and 10am–6pm on Saturday. There is another central post office located on place du 16 Novembre in Guéliz, open 8am–4pm Monday to Friday. Most shops that sell postcards also sell stamps.

Weather

Marrakech is warm all year round, although January and February have rainfall, with the temperatures dropping during the nights. The summer heat is at its most oppressive and fierce in July and August.

The best times to visit are March to June and September to December. The peak tourist season is Easter and Christmas/New Year, so be sure to make reservations well ahead in order to secure a room if you plan to visit during these periods.

Opening Hours

Although a Muslim country, much of Morocco follows a Monday to Friday working week. Business hours for banks are 8:15am–3:45pm Monday to Friday (9:30am–2pm during Ramadan). Shops open a bit later but stay open until 8pm or 9pm. On Fridays, shops in the souks shut at lunch.

During the religious festivals of Eid El Fitr and Eid El Adha, the city stays shut for a minimum of two days, so travelling is very difficult. In the holy month of Ramadan (begins 22 March in 2023 and 10 March in 2024, and lasts for 30 days) many Muslims fast during the day; due to this, many restaurants and eateries are closed until sundown. Some restaurants may also abstain from serving alcohol at this time.

COVID-19 Increased rates of infection may result in temporary opening hours and/or closures. Always check ahead before visiting museums, attractions and hospitality venues.

Visitor Information

The **Regional Tourist Office**, open 8:30am–4:30pm Monday to Friday, is near the Marché Central in Guéliz. However, it is not always particularly useful and chances are you will find that the staff at your accommodation will be of more help.

Trips and Tours

You may be approached in the Medina by people offering their services as guides. Always check that they are licensed before hiring them. Any discount that a guide may obtain for you at shops will be negated by their own commission, which the shopkeeper will factor into the price of goods, so be sure to bargain when making purchases. Your hotel can organize an official guide for you. Alternatively try booking with a reputable company such as **Travel Link** or **Marrakech Guided Tours**.

Numerous companies offer Morocco packages and most of them include stays in Marrakesh. **Best of Morocco** is UK-based; **Marrakesh Voyage** is US-based; **Real Morocco Tours** is a reputable Marrakech-based Amazigh-run operator with an array of packages.

Local Customs

Islam is the state religion and the king of Morocco is the leader of the faithful. It is therefore considered in bad taste to criticize religion. It is also ill-mannered to disturb someone while they are at prayer. Non-Muslims are not allowed inside mosques and saintly shrines. As in all Muslim countries, visitors to Morocco should dress modestly and refrain from overt signs of affection in public.

Alcohol is frowned upon by Islam. However, hotels and restaurants with a predominantly international clientele are allowed some flexibility. It is above all during Ramadan that certain rules must be obeyed. The fast of Ramadan is strictly observed in Morocco, and many dining establishments close during daylight hours as a result. Non-Muslims should avoid eating, drinking and smoking in public during the day.

The Indigenous people of North Africa, known as Berbers throughout most of history, prefer to call themselves Amazigh, meaning "free people". The name "Berber" was given to the Amazigh people by the Romans, was perpetuated by Arab invaders and used by the French in the early 20th century. The Amazigh people in Morocco continue to agitate for the acknowledgment of their identity and culture, and some progress has been made, including the recognition of their language, Tamazight, as an official language of Morocco in 2011.

Bargaining is a standard process when shopping, but more and more places are moving to fixed prices. When bargaining, offering half or two-thirds of the asking price is a good place to start. If you manage to get a good deal, you may feel that you have undercut the seller – don't worry, they wouldn't sell it if they weren't making a profit.

Language

French and Arabic are the main languages. Tamazight, the language of the Amazigh people, is also used in the city. English is spoken widely by those working in the tourism industry.

Taxes and Refunds

VAT of 20 per cent is levied on most goods and services. Visitors may be eligible for a refund on presentation of a receipt for purchases of over 2,000 Dh. This service is available at Marrakech airport.

Accommodation

Marrakech has a wealth of accommodation, mainly comprising of riads or *maisons d'hôtes*, a term that roughly translates as "boutique hotels".

A riad (the word originates from the Arabic for "garden") is a house in the Medina with a courtyard. Uniquely Moroccan, they are nearly all privately owned guesthouses and can range from a cosy four rooms to close to 20, from humble to ultra-stylish. It is usually possible to rent a whole riad at a reduced rate. Many riads offer transport to and from the airport: ask about this when making your booking.

All Marrakech's riads are in the Medina. The big international hotels are in Hivernage, between the Medina and the airport – a taxi ride away from Jemaa el Fna. There is also a clutch of super-exclusive luxury hideaways and resorts in the Palmeraie.

High season is Christmas and New Year and the weeks around Easter. Prices can go up by as much as 25 per cent, and that's if you can find a room – you really need to book months in advance. September and October are generally also busy as the worst of the summer heat is over. January and February are low season. Make sure that your chosen accommodation has air conditioning if you are visiting between May and October, and heating in January and February.

Negotiating a lower price for a hotel room is common, and fruitful. At times, it can be possible to obtain reductions of up to 30 per cent. It is a waste of time, however, during the high season.

DIRECTORY

VISITOR INFORMATION

Regional Tourist Office
MAP C5 ◼ Rue Cadi Ayad, Guéliz
ⓦ visitmarrakech.com

TRIPS AND TOURS

Best of Morocco
ⓦ morocco-travel.com

Marrakech Guided Tours
ⓦ marrakechguided tours.com

Marrakesh Voyage
ⓦ marrakesh-voyage. com

Real Morocco Tours
ⓦ realmorocco tours.com

Travel Link
ⓦ travellink.ma

Places to Stay

PRICE CATEGORIES
For a standard, double room per night (with breakfast if included), taxes and extra charges.

(Dh) under 1,200 Dh (Dh)(Dh) 1,200–2,500 Dh
(Dh)(Dh)(Dh) over 2,500 Dh

Luxury Riads and Hotels

El Fenn
MAP J3 ▪ Derb Moulay Abdallah Ben Hezzian, Medina ▪ 0524 44 12 10 ▪ www.el-fenn.com ▪ (Dh)(Dh)(Dh)
Vanessa Branson's A-list riad features stylish suites and private riads sharing four courtyards, a *hammam*, boutique, library, bar and restaurant, three pools and a screening room.

La Maison Arabe
MAP H2 ▪ 1 derb Assehbé, Medina ▪ 0524 38 70 10 ▪ www.lamaisonarabe. com ▪ (Dh)(Dh)(Dh)
The first riad hotel in Morocco remains one of the best. Owned by Prince Fabrizio Ruspoli, it has 26 ornate rooms mixing traditional Moroccan decor with European old world charm. Amenities include a fine restaurant, pool, spa and affiliated country club.

La Mamounia
MAP H5 ▪ Ave Bab Jedid, Medina ▪ 0524 38 86 00 ▪ www.mamounia.com ▪ (Dh)(Dh)(Dh)
A multimillion-dollar renovation reconfirmed the historic La Mamounia's status as arguably the best and most glamorous hotel in North Africa. Smartly dressed non-guests may catch a glimpse of the sumptuous interiors by visiting one of the many restaurants or bars *(see pp34–5)*.

La Sultana
MAP K6 ▪ 403 rue de la Kasbah, Medina ▪ 0524 38 80 08 ▪ www.lasultana hotels.com ▪ (Dh)(Dh)(Dh)
This luxury hotel is discreetly hidden off a courtyard beside the Saadian Tombs. The interiors, a riot of Asian and African styles, are a complete contrast. It's one of the few hotels in the Medina with a decent-sized pool (plus spa).

Le Farnatchi
MAP K2 ▪ 2 derb Farnatchi, Medina ▪ 0524 38 49 10 ▪ www.lefarnatchi.com ▪ (Dh)(Dh)(Dh)
Five houses were remodelled to create ten suites, two courtyards and numerous beautiful public spaces. Moroccan-meets-European in style, while facilities include a restaurant, spa, *hammam* and complimentary *djellabas* (traditional house robes).

Riad Enija
MAP K2 ▪ 9 derb Mesfioui, Medina ▪ 0524 44 09 26 ▪ www.riadenija.com ▪ (Dh)(Dh)(Dh)
Three adjoining houses and a wild garden courtyard make up this striking riad. Rooms verge on the fantastical, with furniture fashioned by international artists. Do you photograph or sleep in the beds?

Riad de Tarabel
MAP J2 ▪ 8 derb Sraghna, Medina ▪ 0524 39 17 06 ▪ www.riad-de-tarabel. com ▪ (Dh)(Dh)(Dh)
French owners have brought a part of Provence to this elegant ten-room riad hidden down a lane by the Dar El Bacha Palace. Delicious lunches and dinners are firmly Moroccan, and the rooftop terrace with views of the Medina. There is a spa on site as well.

Royal Mansour
MAP G3/4 ▪ rue Abou El Abbas Sebti, Medina ▪ 0529 80 80 80 ▪ www.royalmansour.com ▪ (Dh)(Dh)(Dh)
Service at this top hotel begins at the airport, where guests are met and whisked through customs and chauffeured to this exclusive city-centre retreat of mini villas set in manicured gardens. It is the last word in privacy, opulence and VIP treatment, but then it is owned by the King of Morocco.

Villa des Orangers
MAP J5 ▪ 6 rue Sidi Mimoun, Medina ▪ 0524 38 46 38 ▪ www.villadesorangers.com ▪ (Dh)(Dh)(Dh)
A grand residence that once belonged to a judge, this boutique hotel has 27 suites arranged around two beautiful courtyards. The lovely roof terrace has unrivalled views of the Koutoubia.

International Hotels

Ibis Marrakech Centre Gare

MAP B5 ■ Ave Hassan II, Guéliz ■ 0524 43 59 29 ■ www.accorhotels.com ■ (Dh)

A standard Ibis hotel, with 109 air-conditioned, basic but comfortable rooms. There is a garden and pool. The hotel is close to the train station and the long-distance bus station.

Bab Hotel

MAP B5 ■ Cnr blvd Mansour Eddahbi and rue Mohammed El Beqqal, Guéliz ■ 0524 43 52 50 ■ babhotel marrakech.ma/en/ ■ (Dh)(Dh)

A stylish, modern boutique hotel in the New City. Rooms are white and minimalist, kitted out with flatscreen TVs, desks and Nespresso machines. There's a buzzing rooftop bar and ground-floor restaurant.

Le Méridien N'Fis

MAP C7 ■ Ave Mohammed VI, Hivernage ■ 0524 33 94 00 ■ www. lemeridiennfis.com ■ (Dh)(Dh)

A five-minute taxi ride from the Medina. It has 277 rooms, restaurants, a popular nightclub and an excellent spa. The architecture is utilitarian but it does have a nice garden setting.

Mövenpick Mansour Eddahbi Marrakech

MAP C7 ■ Ave Mohammed VI, Hivernage ■ 0524 33 91 00 ■ www.movenpick. com ■ (Dh)(Dh)

The 503 rooms in this large and elegant resort are deocrated in mixed elements of Morroccan and European style. Along with three pools, gardens and a spa there is a kids' club as well as four restaurants.

Radisson Blu

MAP C5 ■ 166–176 ave Mohammed V, Guéliz ■ 0525 07 70 00 ■ www.radisson hotels.com ■ (Dh)(Dh)

Opened in 2016, this hotel is a competitively priced five-star attached to the Carré Eden shopping complex. The hotel has 193 contemporary, high-spec rooms and is a 20-minute walk from the Medina but still central to the many shops, restaurants, bars and entertainment of the New City.

Savoy Le Grand

MAP C6 ■ Ave Prince Moulay Rachid, Hivernage ■ 0524 35 10 00 ■ www.savoyle grandhotel marrakech. com ■ (Dh)(Dh)

A 15-minute walk from the Medina, this is a large, modern, resort-style hotel with wings arcing around a large central swimming pool. It's attractive, well maintained and a very good deal for the price.

Sofitel Marrakech

MAP C6 ■ Rue Harroun Errachid, Hivernage ■ 0524 42 56 00 ■ sofitel. accorhotels.com ■ (Dh)(Dh)

An extremely attractive 207-room property with Moroccan architecture, large, bright rooms and a location right on the doorstep of the Medina. What's more, the excellent Comptoir Darna [see p83] and Table du Marché restaurants are just across the road.

Four Seasons

MAP B6 ■ 1 blvd de la Menara, Hivernage ■ 0524 35 92 00 ■ www. fourseasons.com/ marrakech ■ (Dh)(Dh)

Opened in 2011, the property lies between the Medina and airport, close to the Menara Gardens. It takes the form of a cluster of low-lying rose-coloured buildings set in 16 ha (40 acres) of beautifully landscaped gardens. Service and amenities are top class.

Les Jardins de la Koutoubia

MAP J3 ■ 26 rue de la Koutoubia, Medina ■ 0524 38 88 00 ■ www. lesjardinsdelakoutoubia. com ■ (Dh)(Dh)

Located just steps away from the Koutoubia Mosque, this well-concealed five-star hotel is relatively modern. The rooms are smart and have a wide range of facilities. A swimming pool dominates the central courtyard, while the roof garden has lovely views of the mosque.

Hotel Es Saadi

MAP C6 ■ Rue Ibrahim El Mazini, Hivernage ■ 0524 33 74 00 ■ www. essaadi.com ■ (Dh)(Dh)(Dh)

The Rolling Stones hung out here in the 1960s but the hotel has moved with the times and still feels contemporary and luxurious. Set in extensive gardens, it offers 150 rooms and 90 suites, plus ten villas with private pool. There is also a serene spa.

Mid-Range Riads

Dar Attajmil

MAP J3 ▪ 23 rue Laksour, off rue Sidi El Yamami ▪ 0524 42 69 66 ▪ www. darattajmil.com ▪ (Dh)

A lovely little riad with just four rooms. It's a short meandering walk north of Jemaa el Fna, and convenient for exploring the souks and Mouassine neighbourhood. This is an intimate, friendly place that bears the stamp of its (English-speaking) Italian owner.

Dar Doukkala

MAP H2 ▪ 83 rue Bab Doukkala, Dar El Bacha ▪ 0524 38 34 44 ▪ www.dardoukkala. com ▪ (Dh)(Dh)

Eight rooms and suites in this enchanting *maison d'hôtes* are filled with wonderful period details. Other eccentricities include a wall of lanterns above a small terrace pool. The two suites have private terraces.

Les Jardins de la Medina

MAP K7 ▪ 21 derb Chtouka, Quartier Kasbah ▪ 0524 38 18 51 ▪ www.lesjardins delamedina.com ▪ (Dh)(Dh)

It is not hard to see why a 19th-century prince chose this riad for his residence. Set in luxuriant gardens, this chic establishment has 36 rooms that blend modern amenities with traditional Moroccan splendour. There is also a lovely pool, a *hammam* and regular musical evenings with local musicians.

Riad 72

MAP H2 ▪ 72 Arset Awsel, Bab Doukkala ▪ 0524 38 76 29 ▪ www.riad72.com ▪ (Dh)

This stylish, Italian-owned riad is very Milan-meets-Marrakech. The house is traditional but the furniture is all imported. There is one dramatically large main suite, a smaller suite and five double rooms, plus a solarium and a *hammam*.

Riad Adore

MAP J2 ▪ 94 derb Tizouagrine, Dar El Bacha ▪ 0524 37 77 37 ▪ www. riadadore.com ▪ (Dh)(Dh)

A beautiful ten-room riad created by a French architect, so it's no surprise it's a real looker. It has a spa, swimming pool and library, as well as lovely roof terraces and salons. The location is excellent, right in the thick of the souks.

Riad AnaYela

MAP J1 ▪ 28 derb Zerwal, Bab El Khemis ▪ 0524 38 69 69 ▪ www.anayela.com ▪ (Dh)(Dh)

A 300-year-old house renovated by a German entrepreneur, who has created something quite magical in this far north corner of the Medina. With only five rooms, it feels like a secret retreat, with a grand indoor courtyard with heated pool, and a spacious rooftop terrace.

Riad Al Massarah

MAP H1 ▪ 26 derb Jdid, Bab Doukkala ▪ 0524 38 32 06 ▪ www.riadal massarah.com ▪ (Dh)(Dh)

A bright, six-room riad with rooms on the first floor overlooking a central courtyard with turquoise plunge pool. There's also

a dining room, *hammam*, massage room and library. It has won awards for its environmental and employee welfare policies.

Riad El Mezouar

MAP L3 ▪ 28 derb El Hammam ▪ 0524 38 09 49 ▪ www.riadel mezouar.com ▪ (Dh)(Dh)

A serene, whitewashed riad with a courtyard pool and large rooms fitted with lovely traditional furnishings. Its only slight drawback is the location – a 15-minute walk from Jemaa el Fna.

Riad Kheirredine

MAP H1 ▪ 2 derb Chelligui, Sidi Ben Slimane ▪ 0524 38 63 64 ▪ www.riadkheirredine. com ▪ (Dh)(Dh)

Hidden away up in the north of the Medina, this Italian-managed three-storey riad has 11 gorgeously decorated deluxe rooms and suites. There are two pools, a *hammam* and a spa.

Riad Kniza

MAP G1 ▪ 34 derb L'Hôtel, Bab Doukkala ▪ 0524 37 69 42 ▪ www. riadkniza.com ▪ (Dh)(Dh)

A palatial riad filled with objets d'art. For 35 years its Moroccan antique dealer/owner has been the go-to guide to the city for celebrities, showing around stars such as Tom Cruise and Brad Pitt, and at least one US president.

Riad l'Orangeraie

MAP J2 ▪ 61 rue Sidi El Yamani, Mouassine ▪ 0661 23 87 89 ▪ www. riadorangeraie.com ▪ (Dh)(Dh)

Created by two French brothers, this riad has

seven comfortable rooms set around two courtyards, one of which is planted, the other filled by a sparkling plunge pool. The location is excellent, in the heart of buzzing Mouassine.

Riad Noga

MAP L3 ▪ 78 derb Jdid, Douar Graoua ▪ 0524 37 76 70 ▪ www.riadnoga.com ▪ ⓓ ⓓ

A spacious German-run riad with a homely air and efficient service, it has 11 rooms, three roof terraces and a decent-sized pool, and all the rooms come with TV sets, sound systems and cosy fireplaces for cool nights.

Riad Les Yeux Bleus

MAP H2 ▪ 7 derb El Ferrane, Bab Doukkala ▪ 0524 37 81 61 ▪ www.marrakech-boutique-riad.com ▪ ⓓ ⓓ

Despite the name, the eight beautifully designed guestrooms here are painted various vivid tones of blue, yellow and green. It makes for cheerful surroundings, aided by super-friendly staff and good amenities including two pools, a sun terrace and a library.

Riyad Al Moussika

MAP K3 ▪ 62 derb Boutouil, Kennaria ▪ 0524 38 90 67 ▪ www.riyad-al-moussika.com ▪ ⓓ ⓓ

A beautifully restored and maintained former grandee's home, Al Moussika is especially notable for its good food – including an enormous breakfast spread of eggs, pancakes, pastries and fruit. The *hammam*, pool and roof terrace complete the package.

Talaa 12

MAP K2 ▪ 12 Talaa Ben Youssef ▪ 0524 42 90 45 ▪ www.talaa12.com ▪ ⓓ ⓓ

This contemporary, eight-room riad decorated in a simple and unclut-tered, yet appealing style. The traditional feel that permeates the place is augmented by modern comforts such as air conditioning and a *hammam*. It is located right on the doorstep of the souks.

Riad Noir d'Ivoire

MAP K3 ▪ 31–33 derb Jdid, Bab Doukkala ▪ 0524 38 09 75 ▪ www.noir-d-ivoire.com ▪ ⓓ ⓓ ⓓ

In terms of decor, this is something else: a playful and eccentric take on modern Moroccan. Combine two courtyards with plunge pools, a gym, spa, boutique, restaurant with wine cellar, as well as a dinky cocktail bar for one of the hippest places to stay in town.

Budget Riads and Hostels

Chambres d'Amis

MAP K3 ▪ 46/47 derb Moulay Abdelkader, off derb Dabachi, Medina ▪ 0524 42 69 65 ▪ www.chambresdamis.com ▪ ⓓ

A beautiful feminine riad owned and fashioned by Dutch interior designer Anke van der Pluijm. The six guestrooms are lively with colourful kitsch and craftwork, and there's a courtyard garden and roof terrace. Staff can organise cookery and crochet classes, and even bird-watching outings.

Riad Linda

MAP K4 ▪ 93 derb Jamma, Medina ▪ 0524 42 96 07 ▪ www.riadlinda.com ▪ ⓓ

Located close to the city centre, this small riad has six rooms set around a courtyard. The warm and welcoming staff speak English.

Hotel Ali

MAP J4 ▪ Rue Moulay Ismail, Medina ▪ 0524 44 49 79 ▪ No credit cards ▪ ⓓ

A popular launch pad for trips to the Atlas Mountains, this is one of the busiest budget hotels in town. The rooms are a bit of a mixed bag, so inspect a few prior to making your final choice. There's also a rooftop terrace offering superb Medina views.

Hotel du Trésor

MAP J3 ▪ 7 Sidi Boulokat, off Riad Zitoun Kedim, Medina ▪ 0524 37 51 13 ▪ www.hotel-du-tresor.hotelsmarrakech.net ▪ No credit cards ▪ ⓓ

Close to the main square, this little gem of a hotel. It has been around since the early 1950s and its 14 guestrooms, plunge pool and salon retain a retro feel. You could imagine Paul Bowles *(see p44)* hanging out in the salon here.

Hotel Farouk

MAP B5 ▪ 66 ave Hassan II, Guéliz ▪ 0524 43 19 89 ▪ www.hotelfarouk.com ▪ ⓓ

This is one of the best budget options for anyone looking to stay close to the New City. Rooms vary greatly, so check out a few before choosing. All of the rooms are en-suite.

For a key to hotel price categories see p112

Rodamon Riad
MAP K1 ■ Amssafah 32, Medina ■ 0524 37 89 78 ■ www.rodamonhostels.com/marrakech-hostel ■ ⓓⓗ

This large hostel in the Medina features a central swimming pool, dorm-style accommodations, and private rooms. It's a great place to meet other travellers.

Riad Khabia
MAP L6 ■ 6 derb Chtouka, Berrima, Medina ■ 0524 37 59 89 ■ www.riad khabia.com ■ ⓓⓗ

A 15-minute walk from Jemma el Fna, this simple riad is set in a quiet spot of the Medina. It has seven comfortable rooms, an outdoor pool and a *hammam*. In the evening, you can dine on traditional Moroccan dishes while enjoying views from the rooftop terrace.

Hotel Sherazade
MAP K4 ■ 3 derb Djama, Medina ■ 0524 42 93 05 ■ www.hotelsherazade.com ■ ⓓⓗ

This hotel offers a wide range of rooms, from mini-apartments to simple rooms with shared bathrooms. It has a lovely tiled courtyard and an extensive roof terrace with a tent area for dining.

Les Jardins de Mouassine
MAP J3 ■ 20 derb Chorfa El Kebir, Mouassine, Medina ■ 0620 81 53 26 ■ www.lesjardinsde mouassine.com ■ ⓓⓗ

This hotel offers some of the style and charm of the more expensive riads but with the option of competitively priced, hotel-style

double rooms. Facilities include a library, bar, plunge pool, *hammam* and a barbecue grill on the terrace. Cots are also available on request.

Stork Marrakech Luxury Hostel
MAP K5 ■ 113 rue Bab Berrima, Medina ■ 0656 47 45 14 ■ www.stork marrakech.com ■ ⓓⓗ

Located next to Badii Palace, this hostel has rooms that can accommodate four, five, six or eight bunks; single rooms are also available. All rooms have heating and air conditioning. Bathroom and shower facilities are shared. Start the day with breakfast on the rooftop terrace while admiring the view. The hostel offers day trips and activities, including bike tours, souk tours, desert adventures and cooking classes.

Riad Altair
MAP H2 ■ 21 derb Zaouia, Bab Doukkala, Medina ■ 0524 38 52 24 ■ www.riadaltair.com ■ ⓓⓗ

Close to the Bab Doukkala mosque, this is an intimate little riad with six elegant rooms, a games room and library. While there is no restaurant, there is a kitchen and meals can be taken al fresco on the pleasant roof terrace.

Riad Berbère
MAP K2 ■ 23 derb Sidi Ahmed Ben Nasser, off Kaat Benahid, Medina ■ 0524 38 19 10 ■ www.leriadberbere.com ■ ⓓⓗ

A beautiful, light-filled 17th-century riad, sensitively renovated in an elegant, minimalist style. It has a lovely planted central courtyard with

ornamental swimming pool. There is a small *hammam* and staff can organize cooking lessons, yoga sessions and day trips out of town. Cheaper rooms are available.

Riad Jnane Mogador
MAP K4 ■ 116 rue Riad Zitoun El Kedim, derb Sidi Bouloukat, Medina ■ 0524 42 63 23 ■ www.jnanemogador.com ■ ⓓⓗ

A restored 19th-century residence that falls between a riad and hotel, it has 17 rooms around a central courtyard with a fountain and grand staircase. The decor may lack sophistication, but it also has a spa and is good value for money.

Riad Nejma Lounge
MAP G1 ■ 45 derb Sidi M'hamed El Haj, Bab Doukkala ■ 0644 48 57 87 ■ www.riadnejmalounge.morocco-ma.website ■ ⓓⓗ

With six rooms decked out in striking colours, this is one of the funkiest riads in town. A plunge pool in the courtyard and a roof terrace add to its "loungey" feel.

Riad Tizwa
MAP J2 ■ 26 derb El Guerraba, Riad Laarous, Medina ■ 07973 115 471 (UK) or 310 854 2834 (US) ■ www.riadtizwa.com ■ ⓓⓗ

A cool, laid-back and fun English-run riad with a great location in the souks, the Tizwa has six rooms on three floors. There's a small *hammam*, and a pleasant roof terrace for catching the sun, reading books and al fresco dining.

Tchaikana

MAP K2 = 25 derb El Ferrane, Quartier Azbest, Medina = 0524 38 51 50 = www.tchaikana.com = (Dh)(Dh)

Close to the Musée de Marrakech, this riad has two suites, two big double rooms, and one smaller double room. Delphine, one half of the friendly Belgian couple who run the place, is an expert in souk shopping. Cheaper rooms are available.

The Palmeraie and Further Afield

Caravanserai

264 Ouled Ben Rahmoune, 40,000 = 0524 30 03 02 = www.caravanserai.ma = (Dh)

A conversion of several village dwellings north of Marrakech, this hotel offers a stunning mud-brick architecture as well as suites with their own pool. There are also lots of terraces and a *hammam*.

Les Deux Tours

Douar Abiad, Palmeraie = 0524 32 95 25 = www.les-deux-tours.com = (Dh)(Dh)

A landmark piece of architecture by Charles Boccara, this is a beautiful walled retreat of inter-connected villas set in lush Andalusian-style gardens with pools and fountains. The softly seductive rooms make lavish use of Boccara's trademark *tadelakt*.

Palmeraie Palace

Circuit de la Palmeraie = 0524 33 43 43 = www.palmeraieresorts.com = (Dh)(Dh)

This large five-star hotel on the northern edge of the Palmeraie, with a golf course attached, also has pools, gardens, tennis courts, restaurants and a popular nightclub.

Amanjena

Km 12, route de Ouarzazate = 0524 39 90 00 = www.aman.com = (Dh)(Dh)(Dh)

Part of the ultra-exclusive Amanresorts group, the place resembles a film set of an Arabian epic – appropriate given the number of film stars and other A-listers that check in here. Accommodation consists of 39 private villas, some with their own walled gardens.

Fairmont Royal Palm

Km 12, route d'Amizmiz = 0524 48 78 00 = www.fairmont.com/marrakech = (Dh)(Dh)(Dh)

Covering 231 hectares (571 acres) of orange, palm and olive trees, this hotel, located 20 minutes south of the city centre, will have strong appeal to two groups: spa fanatics and golfers. The former are catered for with an enormous spa, the latter by the Royal Palm Golf Club.

Jnane Tamsna

Douar Abiad, Palmeraie = 0524 32 84 84 = www.jnanetamsna.com = (Dh)(Dh)(Dh)

This coolest and most elegant of the Palmeraie villas has featured in magazines but there's plenty of substance here too – surrounding fruit orchards, and vegetable and herb gardens provide the all-organic produce for the kitchen. Cheaper rooms are available.

Ksar Char-Bagh

Jnane Abiad, Palmeraie = 0524 32 92 44 = www.ksarcharbagh.fr = (Dh)(Dh)(Dh)

This Marrakech hotel is a re-creation of an Alhambran palace court on a grand scale. It's all about excess – from the heated pool to the cigar salon. The hotel will pick up guests from the airport in old London taxis.

Mandarin Oriental

Route du Golf Royal = 0524 29 88 88 = www.mandarinoriental.com/marrakech = (Dh)(Dh)(Dh)

Opened in 2015, the Mandarin has 54 single-storey villas, all with private pools, in a beautiful garden ten-minutes' drive southeast of the Medina. Expect top-class facilities including three restaurants, indoor and outdoor swimming pools, a spa and access to two golf courses.

Palais Namaskar

Route de Bab Atlas, Palmeraie = 0524 29 98 00 = www.palaisnamaskar.com = (Dh)(Dh)(Dh)

The Namaskar is a grand property located 20 minutes northeast of the Medina in the Palmeraie. It combines grand architecture and vistas with landscaped grounds, super-spacious rooms and suites, and a full-service spa as well as yoga and fitness centres. If you are not a guest, it is worth visiting just for the rooftop No Mad Bar with its views of the Atlas Mountains.

For a key to hotel price categories see p112

General Index

Acknowledgments

This edition updated by

Contributor Amanda Mouttaki
Senior Editor Alison McGill
Senior Designer Vinita Venugopal
Project Editor Dipika Dasgupta
Editor Anuroop Sanwalia
Picture Research Administrator
Vagisha Pushp
Publishing Assistant Halima Mohammed
Picture Research Manager Taiyaba Khatoon
Jacket Designer Jordan Lambley
Cartographer Ashif
Cartography Manager Suresh Kumar
DTP Designer Rohit Rojal
Senior Production Editor Jason Little
Production Controller Kariss Ainsworth
Deputy Managing Editor Beverly Smart
Managing Editors Shikha Kulkarni,
Hollie Teague
Managing Art Editor Sarah Snelling
Senior Managing Art Editor Priyanka Thakur
Art Director Maxine Pedliham
Publishing Director Georgina Dee

DK would like to thank the following for
their contribution to the previous editions:
Kathryn Glendenning, Andrew Humphreys,
Alan Keohane, Mary Novakovich,
Helen Peters

The publisher would like to thank the
following for their kind permission to
reproduce their photographs:

Key: a-above; b-below/bottom; c-centre; f-far;
l-left; r-right; t-top

123RF.com: Tudor Antonel Adrian 11crb;
Birgit Korber 32bc; Pulpitis 19br; Oleg
Seleznev 16-7.

33 rue Majorelle: 82cla.

4Corners: SIME/Paolo Giocoso 14-5.

Alamy Stock Photo: AA World Travel Library
79br, 80tl; AF archive 34bl; Africa 79t; AGE
Fotostock 99br; Bon Appetit 58br; Paul
Carstairs 88cb; Ian Dagnall 67cra; Dbimages
96clb; PE Forsberg 96tr; Kevin Foy 17tl, 52tr;
FreeProd 18t; Adam Goodwin 13br; Grant
Rooney Premium 14clb; Hemis 3tr, 52clb,
68cla, 76cb, 104-5; Idealink Photography 53b;
imageBROKER 11cl, 35tr; Images & Stories
70t; Image Professionals GmbH / Elan
Fleisher 49crb; JAM WORLD IMAGES 29bl,
M.Sobreira 77crb; Franck Jeannin 84-5;
Shirley Kilpatrick 13br; Art Kowalsky 67b;
Alistair Laming 10br; Mark Lees 78tl; Rob
Matthews 20cla; ilpo musto 57cr; Eric Nathan
20bc; Olga Popkova 59tr; Quantum Pictures
22-3, 66cla; Robertharding 2tl, 3tl, 8-9, 35crb,
64-5; Grant Rooney 54t, 93br; Shoults 38cla;
M.Sobreira 77crb; Dave Stamboulis 87bl; Paul
Strawson 86cla; Kevin Su 100tr; Sebastian
Wasek 31br; Tim E White 56clb, 76cla; Jan
Wlodarczyk 1, 4crb, 50tl, 88t; Andrew Woodley
12br, 30cl; Patrizia Wyss 13tl.

AWL Images: Mauricio Abreu 58tl.

Comptoir Darna: 60b.

Dar Al Hossoun: Dominique Larosière 51crb.

Dar Daïf: 103cr.

David Bloch Gallery: 42tl.

Dreamstime.com: Tudor Antonel Adrian 80b;
Dbajurin 4b; Devy 12cl; Dorinmarius 7cra;
Rene Drouyer 11c; Flavijus 19tr; Freeshot
24-5; Abdul Sami Haqqani 25tl; Jahmaican
21tr; Javarman 10cl, 100b; Kemaltaner 4cl;
Sergii Koval 59cl; Karol Kozlowski 50b, 62tr,
75cl; Madrugaderde 10cr; Marat Iakhin
34-5c; Masar1920 20-1; Giuseppe Masci 32-3;
Mbasil 6cla; Paweł Opaska 102cla; Piotr
Pawinski 4clb; Pipa100 29tl; Andrea Poole
81cla; Ppy2010ha 59bc; Sspezi 17bl; Adriana
Stampfl 42crb; Simon Thomas 18cb; Anibal
Trejo 28-9, 30br, 31clb; Sergii Velychko 30-1;
Sarah Wilkie 98tl; Witr 99t; Yakthai 10bl.

Dunes & Desert: 55br.

Getty Images: Glen Allison 92tl; Charles
Bowman 89crb; Bartosz Hadyniak 93t;
Simeone Huber 101cl; Hulton Archive / H. F.
Davis 35c; The Image Bank Unreleased /
Laurie Noble 25br; Ipsumpix 38b; The John
Deakin Archive 39tr; Kelly Cheng Travel
Photography 74br; Jason Kempin 43br; Izzet
Keribar 74t; Jean-Pierre Lescourret 40tr;
61crb; Lonely Planet 46bl, 54bc; 72cla;
Moment / Karl Hendon 27tc; Laurie Noble
73tr; Richard T. Nowitz 28clb, 40b; Sergio
Pitamitz 15tl; Massimo Pizzotti 68b; Reporters
Associes 39cl; Robertharding / Matthew
Williams-Ellis 32cl; Abdelhak Senna 33tl;
Paul A. Souders 12c; Mark Thomas 29crb;
Yvan Travert 87tr.

Hammam de La Rose: 44-5.

Hotel Villa Maroc: 91t.

iStockphoto.com: aroundtheworld.
photography 15crb; Fafou 24clb;
FrankvandenBergh 41tr; E+ / Pavliha 4t,
10cla; GuyBerresfordPhotography 19clb;
Bartosz Hadyniak 102b; Lukasz Janyst 7tr;
javarman3 41cl; Sylwia Kania 94-5; Zdenek
Last 58c; Olena_Z 26br; RAndrey 11tr;
Elzbieta Sekowska 33cr.

**Kasbah du Toubkal (www.kasbahdutoubkal.
com):** Alan Keohane 63b.

Kasbah Tamadot: 97br.

Kechmara: 83br.

La Mamounia: 11bl, 35bl, 67cra.

La Sultana Hotels: 47t.

Le Foundouk: 60tl.

Maison de la Photographie: 43tl.

Maison Tiskiwin: 69tl.

Nikki Beach: 57b.

Oasiria: 55cl.

Pepe Nero: 71cr.

Riad Farnatchi: 48br.

Riad Kniza: 2tr, 4cr, 36-7, 48t.

Robert Harding Picture Library: Ethel Davies 94tl; Lee Frost 16clb; Christian Kober 63tr.

Shutterstock.com: byvalet 26-27c; saiko3p 27crb; Todamo 4cla.

Taros: 90br.

Cover

Front and spine: **Alamy Stock Photo:** Jan Wlodarczyk.

Back: **Alamy Stock Photo:** © Bill Bachmann cl, Jan Wlodarczyk b, crb; **Dreamstime.com:** Prakich Treetasayuth tr; **iStockphoto.com:** GuyBerresfordPhotography tl.

Pull Out Map Cover

Alamy Stock Photo: Jan Wlodarczyk.

All other images © Dorling Kindersley.

For further information see:
www.dkimages.com.

Penguin
Random
House

First edition 2008

Published in Great Britain by
Dorling Kindersley Limited
DK, One Embassy Gardens, 8 Viaduct
Gardens, London SW11 7BW, UK

The authorised representative in the EEA is
Dorling Kindersley Verlag GmbH. Arnulfstr.
124, 80636 Munich, Germany

Published in the United States by
DK Publishing, 1745 Broadway, 20th Floor,
New York, NY 10019, USA

Copyright © 2008, 2022 Dorling
Kindersley Limited
A Penguin Random House Company

22 23 24 25 10 9 8 7 6 5 4 3 2 1

A CIP catalogue record is available
from the British Library.

A catalogue record for this book is available
from the Library of Congress.

ISSN 1479-344X
ISBN 978-0-2415-6886-6

Printed and bound in China

www.dk.com

*As a guide to abbreviations in visitor information blocks: **Adm** = admission charge; **D** = dinner; **L** = lunch.*

MIX
Paper from
responsible sources
FSC® C018179

This book was made with Forest
Stewardship Council ™ certified
paper – one small step in DK's
commitment to a sustainable future.
For more information go to
www.dk.com/our-green-pledge

Phrase Book: French

In Emergency

Help!	Au secours!	oh sekoor
Stop!	Arrêtez!	aret-ay
Call a doctor!	Appelez un médecin!	apuh-lay uñ medsañ
Call an ambulance!	Appelez une ambulance!	apuh-lay oon oñboo-loñs
Call the police!	Appelez la police!	apuh-lay lah poh-lees
Call the fire brigade!	Appelez les pompiers!	apuh-lay leh poñ-peeyay

Communication Essentials

Yes/No	Oui/Non	wee/noñ
Please	S'il vous plaît	seel voo play
Thank you	Merci	mer say
Excuse me	Excusez-moi	exkoo-zay mwah
Hello	Bonjour	boñzhoor
Goodbye	Au revoir	oh roh-vwar
Good evening	Bonsoir	boñ-swar
What?	Quoi?	kwah
When?	Quand?	koñ
Why?	Pourquoi?	poor-kwah
Where?	Où?	oo

Useful Phrases

How are you?	Comment allez-vous?	kom-moñ talay voo
Very well, thank you.	Très bien	treh byañ
Pleased to meet you.	Enchanté	oñshoñ-tay
Where is/are…?	Où est/sont…?	oo ay/soñ
Which way to…?	Quelle est la direction pour…?	kel ay lah deer-ek-syoñ poor
Do you speak English?	Parlez-vous anglais?	par-lay voo oñg-lay
I don't understand.	Je ne comprends pas.	zhuh nuh kom-proñ pah
I'm sorry.	Excusez-moi.	exkoo-zay mwah

Useful Words

big	grand	groñ
small	petit	puh-tee
hot	chaud	show
cold	froid	frwah
good	bon	boñ
bad	mauvais	moh-veh
open	ouvert	oo-ver
closed	fermé	fer-meh
left	gauche	gohsh
right	droite	drwaht
entrance	l'entrée	l'on-tray
exit	la sortie	sor-tee
toilet	les toilettes	twah-let

Shopping

How much does this cost?	C'est combien s'il vous plaît?	say kom-byañ seel voo play
I would like …	Je voudrais…	zhuh voo-dray
Do you have?	Est-ce que vous avez?	es-kuh voo zavay
Do you take credit cards?	Est-ce que vous acceptez les cartes de crédit?	es-kuh voo zaksept-ay leh kart duh kreh-dee

What time do you open?	A quelle heure êtes-vous ouvert?	ah kel urr et voo oo-ver
What time do you close?	A quelle heure êtes-vous fermé?	ah kel urr et voo fer-may
This one.	Celui-ci.	suhl-wee-see
That one.	Celui-là.	suhl-wee-lah
expensive	cher	shehr
cheap	pas cher, bon marché	pah shehr, boñ mar-shay
size, clothes	la taille	tye
size, shoes	la pointure	pwañ-tur
white	blanc	bloñ
black	noir	nwahr
red	rouge	roozh
yellow	jaune	zhohwn
green	vert	vehr
blue	bleu	bluh

Types of Shop

antique shop	le magasin d'antiquités	maga-zañ d'oñteekee-tay
bakery	la boulangerie	booloñ-zhuree
bank	la banque	boñk
bookshop	la librairie	lee-brehree
cake shop	la pâtisserie	patee-sree
cheese shop	la fromagerie	fromazh-ree
chemist	la pharmacie	farmah-see
department store	le grand magasin	groñ maga-zañ
delicatessen	l'épicerie	lay-pee-sree
gift shop	le magasin de cadeaux	maga-zañ duh kadoh
greengrocer	le marchand de légumes	mar-shoñ duh lay-goom
grocery	l'alimentation	alee-moñta-syoñ
market	le marché	marsh-ay
newsagent	le magasin de journaux	maga-zañ duh zhoor-no
post office	la poste, le bureau de poste, le PTT	pohst, booroh duh pohst, peh-teh-teh
supermarket	le supermarché	soo pehr-marshay
tobacconist	le tabac	tabah
travel agent	l'agence de voyages	l'azhoñs duh vwayazh

Sightseeing

art gallery	la galerie d'art	galer-ree dart
bus station	la gare routière	gahr roo-tee-yehr
church	l'église	l'aygleez
garden	le jardin	zhar-dañ
library	la bibliothèque	beebleeo-tek
mosque	la mosquée	mos-qay
museum	le musée	moo-zay
railway station	la gare	gahr
tourist information office	renseignements touristiques, le syndicat d'initiative	roñsayn-moñ toorees-teek, sandee-ka d'eenee-syateev

Staying in a Hotel

Do you have a vacant room?	Est-ce que vous avez une chambre?	es-kuh voo-zavay oon shambr
double room, with double bed	chambre à deux personnes, avec un grand lit	shambr ah duh pehr-son, avek un groññ lee
twin room	chambre à deux lits	shambr ah duh lee

single room	chambre à	shambr ah
	une personne	oon pehr-son
room with a	chambre avec	shambr avek
bath, shower	salle de bains,	sal duh bañ,
	une douche	oon doosh
I have a	J'ai fait une	zhay fay oon
reservation.	réservation.	rayzehrva-syoñ

Eating Out

Have you	Avez-vous une	avay-voo oon
got a table?	table libre?	tahbl duh leebr
I want to	Je voudrais	zhuh voo-dray
reserve	réserver	rayzehr-vay
a table.	une table.	oon tahbl
The bill	L'addition s'il	l'adee-syoñ seel
please.	vous plaît.	voo play
I am a	Je suis	zhuh swee
vegetarian.	végétarien.	vezhay-tehryañ
waitress/	Madame,	mah-dam,
waiter	Mademoiselle/	mah-
	Monsieur	demwahzel/
		muh-syuh
menu	le menu,	men-oo, kart
	la carte	
fixed-price	le menu à	men-oo ah
menu	prix fixe	pree feeks
cover charge	le couvert	koo-vehr
wine list	la carte des vins	kart-deh vañ
glass	le verre	vehr
bottle	la bouteille	boo-tay
knife	le couteau	koo-toh
fork	la fourchette	for-shet
spoon	la cuillère	kwee-yehr
breakfast	le petit	puh-tee
	déjeuner	deh-zhuh-nay
lunch	le déjeuner	deh-zhuh-nay
dinner	le dîner	dee-nay
main course	le plat principal	plah prañsee-pal
starter, first	l'entrée, le hors	l'oñ-tray, or-
course	d'oeuvre	duhvr
dish of the day	le plat du jour	plah doo zhoor
café	le café	ka-fay

Menu Decoder

baked	cuit au four	kweet oh foor
beef	le boeuf	buhf
beer	la bière	bee-yehr
boiled	bouilli	boo-yee
bread	le pain	pan
butter	le beurre	burr
cake	le gâteau	gah-toh
cheese	le fromage	from-azh
chicken	le poulet	poo-lay
chips	les frites	freet
chocolate	le chocolat	shoko-lah
coffee	le café	kah-fay
dessert	le dessert	deh-ser
egg	l'oeuf	l'uf
fish	le poisson	pwah-ssoñ
fresh fruit	le fruit frais	frwee freh
garlic	l'ail	l'eye
grilled	grillé	gree-yay
ice, ice cream	la glace	glas
lamb	l'agneau	l'anyoh
lemon	le citron	see-troñ
meat	la viande	vee-yand
milk	le lait	leh
mineral water	l'eau	l'oh
	minérale	meeney-ral
oil	l'huile	l'weel
onions	les oignons	leh zonyoñ
fresh orange	l'orange	l'oroñzh presseh
juice	pressée	

fresh lemon	le citron	see-troñ presseh
juice	pressé	
pepper	le poivre	pwavr
potatoes	les pommes	pom-duh tehr
	de terre	
prawns	les crevettes	kruh-vet
rice	le riz	ree
roast	rôti	row-tee
salt	le sel	sel
sausage	la saucisse	sohsees
seafood	les fruits	frwee duh mer
	de mer	
shellfish	les crustacés	kroos-ta-say
soup	la soupe,	soop,
	le potage	poh-tazh
steak	le bifteck,	beef-tek,
	le steack	stek
sugar	le sucre	sookr
tea	le thé	tay
vegetables	les légumes	lay-goom
vinegar	le vinaigre	veenaygr
water	l'eau	l'oh
red wine	le vin rouge	vañ roozh
white wine	le vin blanc	vañ bloñ

Numbers

0	zéro	zeh-roh
1	un, une	uñ, oon
2	deux	duh
3	trois	trwah
4	quatre	katr
5	cinq	sañk
6	six	sees
7	sept	set
8	huit	weet
9	neuf	nerf
10	dix	dees
11	onze	oñz
12	douze	dooz
13	treize	trehz
14	quatorze	katorz
15	quinze	kañz
16	seize	sehz
17	dix-sept	dees-set
18	dix-huit	dees-weet
19	dix-neuf	dees-nerf
20	vingt	vañ
30	trente	tront
40	quarante	karoñt
50	cinquante	sañkoñt
60	soixante	swasoñt
70	soixante-dix	swasoñt-dees
80	quatre-vingt	katr-vañ
90	quatre-	katr-vañ-dees
	vingt-dix	
100	cent	soñ
1,000	mille	meel

Time

one minute	une minute	oon mee-noot
one hour	une heure	oon urr
half an hour	une demi-	oon duh-me urr
	heure	
one day	un jour	un zhorr
Monday	lundi	luñ-dee
Tuesday	mardi	mar-dee
Wednesday	mercredi	mehrkruh-dee
Thursday	jeudi	zhuh-dee
Friday	vendredi	voñdruh-dee
Saturday	samedi	sam-dee
Sunday	dimanche	dee-moñsh

Arabic

Moroccan Arabic is unique to Morocco and is not understood by other Arabic speakers. Moroccans speak faster and abbreviate words. Pronunciation is gentler due to the influence of French.

Useful Words and Phrases

Yes	**Na-am**
No	**Laa**
Hello / Peace be upon you	**Selaam**
Goodbye	**Ma'eel salaama**
Excuse me	**Min fadlak**
Sorry	**Esme'hlee**
Thank you	**Se'hha**
Please	**Min fadlak**
Good morning	**Esbe'h elkheer**
Good evening	**Masaal kheer**
How are you?	**Washraak?**
I'm fine	**Laabas**
I don't understand	**Ana mafhimtaksh**
Do you speak English?	**Tatkalam engleeze-ya?**
God willing	**Inshaala**
big	**kbeer**
small	**sgeer**
hot	**sokhoon**
cold	**baared**
bad	**mashemlee'ha**
good	**mlee'ha**
open	**maftoo'h**
closed	**maghlook**
toilet	**towalett**
a little	**kaleel**
a lot	**bizzaaf**

Emergencies

Stop!	**Owkof!**
Can you call a doctor?	**Momkin kellem el tabeeb?**
Can you call the police?	**Momkin kellem el polees?**

Making a Telephone Call

I'd like to speak to…	**Begheet nekallam…**
This is…	**Hadi…**
Please say… called	**Min fadlak kollo… etkallam**

In a Hotel

Do you have a room?	**Enta 'andak ghorfa?**
With bathroom	**Ma'al 'ham-maam**
single room	**ghorfa le shakhs waa'hid**
double room	**ghorfa le shakhsayn**
shower	**doosh**
key	**meftaa'h**

Shopping

How much is it?	**Kam else'er?**
I'd like…	**Ana 'habbayt**
This one	**Hadi**
That's too much	**Hadi ghaalya**
I'll take it	**Naakhodha**
market	**marshee**
expensive, cheap	**ghaalya, rekheesa**

Sightseeing

art gallery	**galiree daar**
beach	**bhar**
bus station	**stasyon do boos**
entrance	**dokhool**
exit	**khrooj**
garden	**eljonayna**
guide	**geed**
map	**kaart**
mosque	**masjid**
museum	**moozi**

park	**baark**
ticket	**tekee**
tourist office	**mektab soyaa'h**
How much is it to…?	**Kam tekal-laf haazi…?**

Eating Out

Have you got a table for…?	**Enta 'andak towla**
Can I have the bill please?	**Te'eteeni elfatoora min fadlak?**

Menu Decoder

tajeen	steamed pot of vegetables with meat, etc
kuskus	hand-made couscous
elbasteela	pastry filled with vegetables and meat, etc
'hreera	soup
kefta	meatballs with herbs
el'hoot	fish
djaaj	chicken
l'hem	meat
legoorn/khodra	vegetables
maa'a	water

Time

today	**el yoom**
yesterday	**el baareh**
tomorrow	**ghadan**
tonight	**felleel**
day	**nehaar**
hour	**sa'aa**
week	**semaana**

Days of the Week

Monday	**el etneen**
Tuesday	**el tlaata**
Wednesday	**el arbe'aa**
Thursday	**el khamees**
Friday	**el jomo'aa**
Saturday	**el sabet**
Sunday	**el a'had**

Numbers

1	**waa'hid**
2	**zooj**
3	**tlaata**
4	**araba'aa**
5	**khamsa**
6	**set-ta**
7	**seba'a**
8	**tmaanya**
9	**tes'aa**
10	**'ashra**
11	**'hdaash**
12	**etnaash**
13	**tlat-taash**
14	**erba-taash**
15	**khmastaash**
16	**set-taash**
17	**sba'ataash**
18	**tmantaash**
19	**tas'ataash**
20	**eshreen**
21	**waa'hid w'eshreen**
30	**tlatheen**
40	**ereb'een**
50	**khamseen**
60	**set-teen**
70	**seb'een**
80	**tmaneen**
90	**tes'een**
100	**meya**

When you see an apostrophe (') in the Arabic, this means that you pronounce the letter after it with a little puff of air.